W9-AHJ-945

Book Publishers Network
P.O. Box 2256
Bothell • WA • 98041
Ph • 425-483-3040
www.bookpublishersnetwork.com

10 9 8 7 6 5 4 3 2 1
Printed in the United States of America

LCCN 2016962968
ISBN   978-1-945271-30-4

Editor: Tom Bowen
Cover Design: Laura Zugzda
Design & Layout: Melissa Vail Coffman

Planning
PURPOSE[FUL]
LIFE

Secrets of Long[evity]

JEANNETTE BAJALIA

BOOK PUBLISHERS NETWORK
Changing the World One Book at a Time

This book is dedicated to all my heroes from the Greatest Generation that ever lived, especially Mr. Olen Levell, who served his God, his country and his family with great conviction and service. It is with great sadness that Olen is no longer with us, but we are forever inspired by him and the other men and women who allowed me into their lives so their memories and legacies live on and we can learn from their great wisdom and patriotism.
They have forever influenced my life and reinforced for me what God put us on earth to do—SERVE ONE ANOTHER unconditionally and with passion and grace.

CONTENTS

Acknowledgements

WHEN I SET OUT TO WRITE THIS BOOK, I thought it was simply going to be a process for me to learn what the Greatest Generation knows, and to take that and transfer it into the life-planning process we use to make sure retirees and pre-retirees are prepared for the long haul—three, four and maybe even five decades of retirement. I never dreamed I would be so touched and influenced by the men and women who allowed me into their homes.

So, my deepest gratitude goes to the individuals and families who shared their lives, their pain, their joys and sorrows. They will never know how blessed I am, and how I feel I am the luckiest woman in the world to have had the opportunity to learn from them. This experience has helped me define who I need to become for the next half of my life. I thought I had learned a lot from my own family responsibilities with aging family members, but what I realized was that I just didn't know enough. For this, I am deeply grateful. So, I can continue on the journey of discovery, and reach out to the multitudes of centenarians and supercentenarians out there, encouraging them to continue living with passion and conviction and to keep on influencing our society-at-large.

I learned much that will help me help my clients, family members, friends and others. I was also touched by the depth of the sorrow they expressed about the state of the country they are leaving to their children, grandchildren and great-grandchildren. We owe it to this great generation to recognize they still have meaningful contributions to make to our society. We can still learn from their wisdom. My thanks go to this group and to the other older adults who are yet to come across my path. I intend to continue my journey of discovery by learning from the Greatest Generation that ever lived.

In addition to the men and women who shared their lives with me, I am thankful to the two individuals who helped me make this book a reality and who encouraged me to "go for it" when this book was simply an idea. It became more, thanks to their encouragement and support. Thank you to my editor and creative confidant Tom Bowen, and to Bill Kentling, founder of the 65669 Writers Guild. They were right there with me, giving me the confidence I needed to represent this generation through their unique experiences and stories. They helped me get comfortable with communicating my passion for serving this generation. Thanks to Bill and Tom, we have just begun!

Thanks also to my staff at Woman's Worth® and Petros Estate & Retirement Planning, who endured my absence from the office and listened to my stories when I came back from my interviews with enthusiasm and excitement. Thank you for your unconditional support and commitment to my vision, and for your leadership in carrying the torch to protect individuals and families. You have never lost sight of the important role you play in doing whatever it takes to help the most senior and vulnerable of all generations.

Finally, I must acknowledge my four sisters, who continue to encourage me despite my lack of availability at family gatherings when work and travel demands interfere. Thank you for understanding that when I am absent from you, it is because I am spending time with seniors who don't have large families like I do, helping them with the affairs of their lives. When my sisters learned about this book, they rolled up their sleeves, cleared the path, and allowed me to follow my heart, my passion and my dream. Your assistance has helped me speak for the men and women in this book and to share their wisdom with the world.

Introduction

OFTEN IN LIFE, WE GET CURVE BALLS, and we never know why God throws them at us. Experiences that seem like dirty deals at the time turn out to be opportunities in disguise. While we are scratching our head, wondering why our life took this or that unexpected direction, we are being groomed. Prepared. Readied to do what we are put here on this earth to do. I believe this.

I know in my case, it was not until I was in my mid-50s that I realized the divine plan for my life—my calling—was that of serving senior citizens and the elderly. Throughout my life, I have been blessed with many amazing opportunities, each of which has prepared me, usually without my realization at the time, for the professional journey that I would eventually take.

COMING TO AMERICA

I was born here, but my parents immigrated to America from a small town in the central West Bank of Palestine called Ramallah, a historically Arab-Christian town located about six miles north of Jerusalem. My mother was 16 years old when her family arranged a marriage with a well-respected young man, Elias Bajalia. My father would learn with a jolt what "family responsibility" meant. His father abandoned him and his mother when he was a teenager, leaving him no choice but to quit school and work in the fields to support his mother. He would develop a deep commitment to family and hard work.

We all love compliments. I beam with pride if someone notices that I am a "hard worker." If such a thing as one's work ethic can be inherited (and I think it can), I am sure I can thank my father's DNA for that. It was by sheer hard work and determination that he could survive and care for the two most important women in his life.

This is the section of the Israeli West Bank wall separating Israel and the historically Christian town of Ramallah, Palestine, my parents' hometown. (Photo by W. Hagens: senadmessage.nl took the picture, for W. Hagens: copyrights have been transferred to him. —Senddamessage.nl, Public Domain, https://commons. wikimedia.org/w/index.php?curid=9533240)

Life in Palestine was hard for my parents. When my older sister, Sue, was 9 months old, my father made a tough decision. He would go to America and establish a homestead, find work, and then send for them. Things didn't work out exactly as he had planned. When he arrived, the United States was in the middle of the Great Depression.

There was trouble back home, as well. Palestine had come under British rule during World War I and, beginning in 1936, Ramallah was at the center of what became known as the Arab Revolt, which lasted until 1939. No sooner had that ended than World War II began. My sister Sue would be 12 years old before my father laid eyes on her again. With the help of relatives, my father in America had made arrangements for relatives to help accompany my mother, sister and grandmother (his mother, whom he had supported since his father abandoned the family) to America via New York City on Aug. 8, 1947. The dream they had both been working for so passionately had finally come true. The adage, "When the dream is big enough, the facts don't count" was a reality with my parents.

A New Beginning

My father established a residence in Jacksonville, Florida, because that's where other relatives who had come from Palestine lived, all of them supporting each other as they made their transition from the "old country" to here. He bought a small home and set up a business making and repairing leather shoes, a skill he had learned in Ramallah. Meanwhile, his young family expanded. Four more daughters were born within four years of his and my mother's reunion. When my twin sisters came along, my father realized that he would not be able to support such a large family on the wages of a cobbler, so he started a restaurant business, and later a retail food operation.

Another major life change he made at the time was giving up smoking cigarettes. He was willing to do whatever it took to support the family additions. When asked what enabled him to give up the habit so easily, he said that he had two new babies (the twins). He said he could "buy milk for them instead of cigarettes for himself." He was selfless like that in all respects.

At the end of his working years, at age 62, he ran a small grocery store.

I am the youngest of five girls. My twin sisters are 15 months older than I and there is a 16-year age gap between the youngest and oldest siblings. In fact, growing up, I felt as if I had two mothers, my mother and my oldest sister, Sue. Sue got married at age 17 when I was 9 months old. The family joke is that I was the only one that didn't get invited to her wedding. As you might suspect, it was another arranged marriage to a man 12 years older than she. After a 59-year marriage and 10 years of commitment to her role as caregiver to her husband when he was severely disabled, Sue was widowed. My older sister is 81 as this book is written in 2016, and is still doing what she loves … catering, and making sure people enjoy her food. She prepares her offerings with heart, spirit and soul. She is a shining example of an individual working purposefully and energetically beyond her 80th birthday, one of many we will hear about in the pages of this book.

LEARNING TO BE A CAREGIVER

Growing up in a multicultural environment, in an extended family, there were constant caregiving responsibilities. Looking back, it is no surprise to me that my values became traditional, and that when growing up, my thoughts went reflexively to taking care of my family. My grandmother lived with us until she died in 1962. I was 11 years old at the time of her death, and I have vivid memories of my mother taking care of her mother-in-law. My grandmother was bedridden from a stroke seven years prior to her death, and was totally dependent on the care we provided in our home. But I do not remember my mother ever complaining. She went about it with a serene and dutiful grace, as if to do otherwise was unthinkable. I never understood the magnitude of this commitment until later in life, when I became a caregiver to my mother and my great-aunt.

My mother became a parent to many in our family and community. At any given time, we could have 10 to 15 "cousins" around the family table. In those days, anyone who was Palestinian and who needed a helping hand was dubbed our "cousin." Three freshly prepared meals were put on the table each day, not just for our immediate and extended family, but for any kids in the neighborhood who had immigrated here with their fathers while their mothers were still back home in the Middle East.

My mother was a teacher. Not in the way you might think. Not with books and lessons. But through her self-lessness, the way she gave so freely of her energy and time, cooked continuously, and took care of my grandmother as an invalid, she taught us all that it was *way* better to give than receive. As the youngest of the daughters, when our "cousins" were at our home playing, my mother would nod at me and I knew what it meant. I should give my toys to other kids. She didn't have to say a word. I knew with a look what she meant. "They didn't have their parents with them in America, and I did." "You have plenty, and they don't." "Your father will replace your toys." And, of course, she was right about all of it.

So, why share all this personal information with you? These childhood experiences were life-defining for me. They marked the beginning of my journey serving others. I believe we are all arrows launched by God's heavenly bow, and sometimes years go by before we land on the target at which He has aimed us. Are those years preparing us to settle well into the role we are meant to play? Perhaps. Is He giving us time to understand and comprehend our life's mission? When I left the corporate world to explore the second chapter of my life, some of my friends asked me if I had completely lost it. I had no logical answer for myself, let alone them. It was as if all the forces of the cosmos were pulling me in that direction.

Until I started the research for this book, I didn't realize just how much I had in common with others whose paths through life were marked by unexplainable turns and illogical switchbacks that made little sense at the time, but were thoroughly understood in hindsight. You will meet many of them in the pages of this book. Some of them are artists who have made their world a brighter, more beautiful place through their gift of music and song. Others touched thousands of lives around with their service. Some have stories to tell that inspire us to persevere.

The people you will meet have one thing in common. They represent a rather happy phenomenon of the 21st century—longevity. Sadly, from the time I began this project, some of the older ones I have interviewed in this book will have passed away. I will tell their stories anyway. Not just because the mark they left on the world is worthy of mention, but because their legacy inspires me to continue. It explains to me why I am so passionate about serving seniors and why I feel such compassion and commitment to relationships, whether they be family, an acquaintance or a client.

Here is a favorite quote of mine, one whose deeper meaning I have grown to appreciate more and more as my arrow has had its flight:

"Each of you should use whatever gift you have received to serve others as faithful stewards of God's grace in its various forms."

– 1 Peter 4:10 (NIV)

CHAPTER I
FINDING THE MARK

"You don't stop laughing when you grow old,
you grow old when you stop laughing."
— George Bernard Shaw

WHEN I WAS 26 YEARS OLD, my father died unexpectedly at age 65. He had never been sick a day in his life. In fact, just a few months before his death, my sisters and I insisted he get a complete physical examination. He put up some resistance, reminding us all how strong and healthy he was. As it turned out, the physical turned up nothing out of the ordinary. He smiled and told us that the doctors had given him a "gold star and a clean bill of health." He died shortly thereafter of a massive heart attack.

While his death was a shock to us all, it was especially emotionally devastating to my mother. He had always been her rock and the sole provider for the family. My great-aunt was also under his care umbrella. Like him, she had immigrated to America with just the clothes on her back. Since she had no other family, my father had assumed full responsibility for her as well.

My father never believed in life insurance—only hard work. "Keep food on the table today, and tomorrow will take care of itself," was his mantra. Thinking about the future was as foreign to him as the country he entered when he immigrated. All he left behind was a $562 monthly Social Security check, a mortgage and responsibility for two women. Not only was his passing an emotional shock to me, but it changed my life dramatically. I had assumed he would live much longer. My grandfather (more about him later in this book) had "lived off the land" past his 100th birthday in an isolated spot near Lake Placid, New York. As the only single daughter with no family responsibility, it fell to me to look after the physical and emotional needs of my mother, who passed away at age 93, and my great-aunt, who lived to be 101.

I would be lying if I said I didn't say, "Why me, Lord?" a few times during that period of time. But, following the example set before me, I soldiered on. Looking back, it was a gift. It gave me hands-on experience with the aging process—something for which I have deep gratitude.

As if that experience wasn't enough to drive the direction of my future, a personal health crisis arrived when I was 36. I was diagnosed with breast cancer. What? How could this be? I was the youngest of five girls with no history of cancer in our family. I didn't have time for this! I was still responsible for two aging family members who needed me. I also had a corporate life. I was in a leadership position with a major insurance company. The job was intense. Several people reported to me. I needed to be there every morning, didn't I? I was quite sure that chaos would ensue if I didn't.

When something like this happens in life, you go through phases. Anger is one of them. I wanted to shake my fist at the heavens and demand an answer, but a healthy respect for God wouldn't let me. So, the anger passed, and when I knew I would recover from the cancer, I decided to take it as another way he was building my character.

I managed to find a cancer treatment protocol that was more in line with my personal values—a metabolic treatment program with a doctor in New York City. Great. I live in Florida. But it was what I needed. As per my usual approach to life, I wanted systemic solutions—not symptomatic solutions, where you just put a bandage on the problem. The cancer treatment program I chose was a lifestyle change and one not covered by insurance. But eventually, it became apparent that I would recover from the cancer. My anger passed. I decided to take all of this misfortune as just another way that God was building my character through adversity.

While I was coping with cancer and its cure, my mother was getting up in years. I wanted to care for her at home if possible. I wanted to treat her the way I knew my father would have—the way I saw her treat my grandmother. Nursing homes were not going to be part of my mother's declining years if I could help it. It just didn't seem congruent with our family's culture. At a cost of $150,000, we added a handicapped-accessible room onto the house for her.

"Why *Me*, Lord?"

We not only learn from the good examples our parents set for us, but we also learn from their mistakes. Because of my father's premature death, and his lack of foresight, I set out to become the consummate planner. Since assuming responsibility for the family at age 26, there was no other way to approach it. I was always anticipating the proverbial "rainy day," and constantly working out strategies to deal with it. One way was by saving money. This was not easy. I had to fund my own health care plan with $2,000 monthly, out of my pocket, while paying for all the care my mother and aunt needed. Add to that the day-to-day expenses of keeping a roof over everyone's head and food on the table.

Again, I sometimes looked up from my budget sheet and stared heavenward as if to ask, "Why me, Lord?" Somehow, with the aid of a calculator and creative financing, I was able to map out a savings strategy. Now, as I look back, those tough times taught me how to prepare and be an expert planner, and I cherish them. Who would have thought that difficult hurdles such as those would spawn planning skills I would need to help others in my second career? I certainly didn't. But I am convinced that's why they were placed in front of me. I truly believe we serve a great God, who has a divinely orchestrated plan for our life. He doesn't get you *to* something if He won't also get you *through* it. Today, I am cancer-free, and I understand clearly the health-wealth connection, which was the essence of my first book, *Wi$e Up Women.*

Hard Work Pays Dividends

I began working with my father in his grocery store at age 7, sweeping floors, stocking shelves, and, when I was old enough to reach the cash register, ringing up customers.

In the 1970s, when I was a young woman, the corporate ladder was just beginning to be extended to women, but not many were climbing it. I seized each rung with enthusiasm and found achievement in the corporate world challenging and thrilling, not to mention financially rewarding.

I went to work for a major insurance company—Prudential—the day after I graduated from high school at the tender age of 16. A university education was out of the question. My father just had no extra money with which to pay for college. After all, I would get married to a good man like my father, wouldn't I? And he would take care of me for the rest of my life, wouldn't he?

I worked hard at my job. By the time I was 21, I had moved into middle management. From there I moved to another insurance giant, Blue Cross and Blue Shield of Florida. I discovered that I could quicken my pace up the corporate ladder with a degree, so I signed up for night classes, majoring in industrial psychology for my undergraduate studies and in human resources management for my master's degree. I was on my way, wasn't I? This was success, wasn't it? I thought so. But God's plans were different. He was preparing me for the next chapter—a career serving seniors as a retirement planning expert where I would integrate health strategies with wealth strategies. That's something I could never have done without the life experiences of both worlds. It is also something I could never have learned out of a book, and it certainly didn't come from any university degree.

LIFE TAKES ANOTHER TURN

In 2007, when my mother passed away and it was only me, I remember thinking that if I had made it this far with the caregiving responsibilities, think of what I could do unfettered. It was the first time since my father had passed away in 1977 that I had only myself to think about. Now, at last, I could focus more on the career that I spent 38 years of my life developing. Now, at last, I could take it to the next level, and seek advancement opportunities that seemed limitless. I had what I thought was a great executive position with Blue Cross Blue Shield Florida (BCBSF). I had a great team of people working under my direction. We were doing purposeful work. The age of health care reform was upon the insurance industry, and we were planning future business models for consumer-driven health plans.

But something wasn't right.

As I went to the office each day, I became less and less satisfied. I remember being asked one day what I did for a living. As I was mouthing the words, "I help an executive team create strategies and tactics to ..." I stopped mid-sentence and couldn't finish. It struck me how ambiguous and empty it sounded to prepare a corporation for a nebulous future. I continued to pretend that I had a satisfying career, only to sink deeper into dissatisfaction, frustration and, as much as I hate to admit it, depression. My job was to motivate others and I was totally de-motivated, with no enthusiasm, passion or energy for what I was doing.

All this came shortly after my mother's death, and I attributed it to the grieving process. I even sought counseling and support, but the feelings didn't go away.

It got to the point that I decided to seek out a spiritual director to help sort it out. I explained to my counselor that I had no longer any enthusiasm or passion for my work, and that was unlike me. I don't give up easily.

"What you lack is a real purpose," my counselor said. "A higher cause."

It was so true. I needed a professional career that would be a means to a more purposeful end.

THE "LEAP OF FAITH"

At age 55, I realized the divine purpose for my life was to serve others. To care for them. My life experiences that led me to this point were just preparation for what was to come. Call it boot camp. All the tough sledding I went through had given me the skills, preparation and capabilities for a higher calling.

But what was I to do? I couldn't just quit work, could I? I had spent more than a quarter-million dollars taking care of family and helping sisters, nieces and nephews, honorary and otherwise, in their times of need. I began weighing my options, pros-and-cons style. I took out a legal pad and began listing the disadvantages of leaving a career I had spent 38 years building. There were several. I was in a pretty healthy defined-benefit plan. I could cash out early, but I knew that if I left the plan before age 62, the depreciation of the pension value would be significant. That was a biggie. I was also at my peak, professionally speaking. I knew my job well, I made an excellent salary, and people I cared about depended on me.

The advantages to leaving were easy to express in three words: I wasn't happy.

I had often used the phrase "leap of faith" in casual conversation, but never knew what those words meant until now. For the first time in my life, I decided to take the risk of retiring from one career without a clue of what my next one would be, or if I would find another. I just knew that, unless I took that step of faith, God could not reveal to me the next chapter in my life. When I made that decision, a wave of peace came over me like a fresh breeze. I didn't have all the facts, but I had faith they would be revealed somehow.

"Be Still"

I had always been a saver, and I had a nice healthy 401(k). Worst-case scenario, if I couldn't figure out how to generate income, I would simply start spending it as I needed to, and recover later. (No, I do not recommend this for you, dear reader.)

I was single. I would take a lump sum payout on my pension. I figured that I could manage my life (and the money) far better than a pension administrator, mainly because I knew I could manage my lifestyle to match my funds.

Besides that, the monthly pension would never adjust for inflation. I confess, however, that I wasn't sure of anything.

My mother passed away in 2006 at the age of 93. I walked away from the corporate world one year later in 2007. Those 12 months were the most life-defining I can recall, because I was on a journey of discovery with my spiritual director. She knew I wanted to resign from my career, but she wanted me to be confident about the move from a spiritual level.

"Be quiet and still for one hour each day," was her advice. I was to do this until I got the "green light" from the depths of my spirit that I was ready to proceed. Each day, for one year, I went to a small chapel and prayed, cried, begged for Godly direction. All I heard in my spirit was that small voice that said, "Be still."

Being still does not come naturally to me. I am one of those individuals who taps her foot at red lights, wanting the cars ahead of me to move. I was so relieved when rotary dial telephones were replaced with touch-tone phones, which made calling faster. Being still is not how I endured the life events that got me here, I reasoned. But, I kept still, only because I had a committed spiritual director who prayed me through the challenges.

I am now convinced "Be still" was a command from God, preparing the way for me to exit without financial pressure. It was then November 2007, and the company I worked for began its operational and business planning cycle for 2008. They decided they needed to cut all operational budgets back 10 percent. When I was consulted as to how to reduce my department's budget, I came up with a marvelous solution that no one expected, not even me. I decided I could merge my department with another one and eliminate my job. This would give me the exit I was looking for (with a nice, healthy severance package), and ensure that none of the people reporting directly to me would lose their jobs. After a few days of negotiating and prodding (just short of begging), my proposal was reluctantly accepted. Reluctantly, because the company felt I was very valuable and wanted me reassigned to another division to continue working on strategic planning. I was flattered, but this was not part of my plan, nor God's plan for me. I was finished in the corporate world and now it was time to discover my next chapter, whatever that was.

SEEKING FINANCIAL HELP

I was free. I left the glass and steel building which had been my prison for so long with a spring in my step and a song in my heart. My first order of business was to get my financial house in order. I had always been a saver. When I began my career in the insurance world, I was just a kid, and I knew little about investing or managing money. When I learned my company was offering a 401(k), I was intrigued.

"What's a 401-Kay?" I asked. It sounded like a vitamin supplement.

I quickly learned that it was a program whereby we could save a portion of our paycheck each week and taxes would be deferred until we retired. Meanwhile, the money would be invested in mutual funds and earn tax-deferred interest. Then the human resources representative explained to me that the company was even willing to match half of what I put in.

"Let me get this straight," I said. "Whenever I make a contribution, you match what I put in, 50 cents on the dollar?" That's essentially it," she said. It didn't take a genius to figure out that the smart thing to do was save every penny I could. I couldn't believe my ears when I learned some of my coworkers wouldn't even participate in the program! I was just miffed at the fact that the government put a cap on how much we could save. It was a no-brainer. The company contribution was free money. Every dollar I saved was a dollar that wasn't taxed. Those untaxed dollars grew untaxed in a market environment that was a win/win situation. In other words, if the stock market went down, my contributions bought more shares of the investments. When the market went back up, those shares increased in value. As long as I was pumping money into the program on a steady basis, I couldn't lose! I contributed as much as I possibly could. When I got a raise, I contributed more. The self-imposed discipline of resisting excessive spending and saving every available dollar paid off. In 38 years, I had managed to save more than $1 million dollars. I also had the lump sum from my pension plan, figuring I could invest it myself and come out better in the long run. I had also converted my 401(k) account to cash as well, knowing full well that, because it was qualified money (the taxes had been deferred), I had 60 days to move it into another qualified account or face an enormous tax bill. I needed some financial advice. I had lots of questions:

- If I could obtain a moderate rate of return, how many years would my money last me without work?
- How much savings would I need to have to comfortably retire?
- What would be my tax obligations in retirement, since everything I had was tax-deferred?
- What could I expect in the way of a guaranteed lifetime income?
- How could I protect myself from unexpected expenses, such as health care?
- What about long-term care?

- Should I pay off my mortgage?
- When should I take Social Security?
- What legal documents did I need to have in place?
- Was I sufficiently insured?
- Were my assets secure?

I had come from a planning background in the corporate world. Now I needed a comprehensive personal financial plan.

I searched for "financial advisors" on Google and saw there were five professional financial advisors (at least that is how their websites advertised them) located within driving distance to my home. I was sure I could find answers to my questions from at least one of them. Also, as an executive with the company, we had access to "the best of the breed" of financial advisors. So, I approached two additional advisors. What a disappointment!

Not one of these "advisors" could answer my questions and offer me a *comprehensive* retirement plan. They all wanted to invest my money for me. Some even showed me colorful pie charts, pointing out how my assets would be "diversified" among small cap stocks, large cap stocks, growth stocks, mutual funds, international investments, and variable annuities. In fact, the portfolio recommendations from all five advisors were essentially the same—cookie-cutter approaches to financial planning. There can be no doubt that investing is an integral part of financial planning, but where was the depth? Where was the road map to my financial future? I felt as if I was a traveler asking for directions to the Interstate and no one knew what an Interstate highway was!

"So let me get this straight," I said to one advisor. "You put all my money in the stock market, and you get to charge me a 2 or 3 percent asset management fee?"

"Yes, that's right. Per year," said the advisor.

"Whether my account goes up or down in value?"

"Yes, that's right."

Well, it wasn't right for me! I wanted more—I wanted a fully integrated plan that protected me the rest of my life.

I must make this point as well. All these advisors were men. As a woman, they didn't treat me with the dignity and respect that I felt I deserved. I felt demoralized and under-valued, not to mention treated like I didn't have a brain cell left in my head. After all, I had managed to save over $1 million while spending an enormous amount on family and caregiving responsibilities, hadn't I? I just had the nagging feeling I was being talked down to, and I didn't like it. They cared more about my money than they did about me or my life-goals.

I think it was after the fifth and final try to communicate with these cookie-cutter advisors that it became abundantly clear: Perhaps *this* was what God wanted me to see. Was he preparing me for a purposeful career in financial services, creating retirement plans for men and women, individuals and families, to make sure their dreams and goals could be achieved with predictability, certainty, and in a way that "does right by people," with dignity and respect?

After my experience, I could see that such a need existed. That need was reinforced when I took an informal poll. I questioned several company executives and asked them what their retirement plan looked like. These were intelligent, educated people. Some were quite accomplished in their field. But, as brilliant as they may have been, and as well remunerated as they were as heads of companies, even these people, as it turned out, did not have a plan—just a bunch of financial products they had been sold.

My "second career" began to take on a recognizable form in my mind—a life of service to seniors. To the best of my ability, I would help them enjoy a life free of financial pressures and help their journey through their life stages with dignity. I would find the tools, strategies and tactics necessary to help them achieve the dreams they had spent lifetimes visualizing.

LIVING PAST 100

"It's starting to get crowded in the 100-year-olds' club," began an article in the *New York Daily News*. The article continued: "Once virtually nonexistent, the world's population of centenarians is projected to reach nearly 6 million by midcentury."

There were only a few thousand people over the age of 100 in 1950, the article said, adding that their numbers are projected to grow by more than 20 times the rates of the total population by 2050, making them the fastest-growing age segment. (*Source: www.nydailynews.com/life-style/centenarians-fastest-growing-age-segment-number-100-year-olds-hit-6-million-2050-article-1.400828*)

Per the United States Census Bureau, life expectancy has increased dramatically for older age groups in recent years. As of 2010, people 90 and older compose 4.7 percent of the older population (age 65 and older), as compared with only 2.8 percent in 1980. By 2050, this share is likely to reach 10 percent. (*Source: www.census.gov/newsroom/releases/archives/aging_population/cb11-194.html*)

The purpose of this book is to share with the reader what it takes to plan for and live beyond 90. It's one thing to plan to live to 75 or 80. It's quite another thing to live beyond 90. Trust me. I know the emotional, physical and financial needs of the 80+ generation. I lived it in my family, and I'm living it daily in my business serving seniors. So, I pray this can help you and your family prepare for the very real possibility that you JUST MAY LIVE TO 100-plus!

CHAPTER II

I'm Going to Live until When?

"The beauty of a woman is not in a facial mole,
but true beauty in a woman is reflected in her soul.
It is the caring that she lovingly gives,
the passion that she knows."

– Audrey Hepburn

I GREW UP IN FLORIDA, a land of tourist attractions. One of
them is the Fountain of Youth. There is no actual fountain of youth, of course. But there is a Fountain of Youth
Archaeological Park located just a few miles from our St.
Augustine office. The full name for the place is Ponce de
Leon's Fountain of Youth Archaeological Park. It is supposed to mark the spot where the Spanish explorer first set
foot on the shores of what would later be the state of Florida in search of, as legend has it, water with rejuvenating
power of eternal youth.

Throughout history, humans have been searching for
some form of a fountain of youth—a magical body of water with the power to cure illnesses and reverse the aging
process. The Greek historian Herodotus wrote about such

a fountain. When Alexander the Great conquered the Persian Empire, he was allegedly looking for these mythical waters. So, get in line, Juan Ponce de Leon. It wasn't an original idea. And for something that never quite panned out, I still congratulate him on remaining quite the local hero. I know at least four statues to Ponce de Leon that grace the streets of St. Augustine.

While there may be no pool of water to splash in for eternal youth, there is a general upturn in longevity and better health these days. We are living longer and better lives in the 21st century. In fact, from the 1900s to date, an astounding 30 years has been added to the average life expectancy, according to some reports. As the kids say, "What's up with that?"

The way life expectancy statistics are calculated, the longer you have lived, the longer you will continue to live—up to a point, of course. So, as pointed out in the previous chapter, more and more Americans are joining the older-than-90 club. What do these folks have in common, if anything? What can we do to keep *our* tickers ticking past the age of 90, and what kind of quality of life can we expect to have physically, emotionally, financially and spiritually if we do? (*Source: http://www.cbsnews.com/news/ living-to-90-and-beyond/*)

That's part of what the research in this book is all about.

THE 90-PLUS STUDY

One of the best explanations of this phenomenon I have ever seen was a two-part report that aired May 4, 2014, by CBS News' *60 Minutes* entitled "Want to Live to 90?" The piece was produced by Shari Finkelstein and featured Lesley Stahl interviewing 90-plus year-old residents of Laguna Woods, California a retirement community, population 14,000. The research behind the show was initiated by

University of California, Irvine in 2003, and involved a $6 million grant from the National Institutes of Health.

"They are called 'the oldest old'," began the *60 Minutes* promo. "They are people age 90 and above, and they are the fastest-growing segment of the U.S. population. Now a landmark study of thousands of members of a retirement community in Southern California is revealing factors that may contribute to living longer. Some of the findings are no surprise—smoking led to shorter lifespans, while those who exercised lived longer. Other findings were unexpected—vitamins did not prolong life, but carrying some extra weight did."

When I watched the show, I was most intrigued by the way Dr. Claudia Kawas of the University of California, Irvine, made the research so understandable to those of us who aren't scientists but are curious about what healthful aging is all about. The study asked thousands of residents in this retirement community, formerly known as "Leisure World," to fill out questionnaires about their diet, activities, vitamin intake, and medical history back in the early 1980s. She and her staff took 14,000 files and sought to determine why certain individuals had died and why some were still alive and well past 90 years of age. Their research zoomed in on 1,600 90-plus residents of Laguna Woods. They were examined physically and cognitively every six months.

FACTORS IN SUCCESSFUL AGING
As you might expect, exercise played a key role in their longer life.

"People who exercised definitely lived longer than people who didn't exercise. As little as 15 minutes a day on average made a difference," reported Dr. Kawas. "Keeping active in nonphysical ways, such as socializing, playing board games, and attending book clubs, also was associated with longer life."

In the *60 Minutes* report, Dr. Kawas told Stahl, "For every hour you spent doing activities in 1981, you increased your longevity, and the benefit of those things never leveled off."

Weight was another key factor, but it may not be exactly what you think.

Kawas told Stahl that being obese at any age is unhealthy. However, she found that older people who were moderately overweight or average weight lived longer than people who were underweight. "It's not good to be skinny when you're old," Dr. Kawas said.

What about vitamins? Alcohol consumption? Her research found that vitamins didn't seem to affect longevity, but alcohol intake did. People who drank up to two drinks per day had a 10-15 percent reduced risk of death compared to nondrinkers.

"A lot of people like to say it's only red wine. In our hands it didn't seem to matter," Dr. Kawas told Stahl.

What about Alzheimer's?

"One of the biggest surprises so far in the study is that 40 percent of the time, what seemed to be Alzheimer's disease in people over 90 actually wasn't. The researchers learned this by studying the brains of the subjects after death; many showed evidence of microscopic strokes," the report said. Kawas told Stahl she had not yet figured out what caused the strokes, so she can't say how to prevent them, but she is still working on it and hopes to discover the causes soon.

A summary of the 90-plus study:

- Genetics are important, but they aren't everything.

- Smokers died earlier than nonsmokers (no surprise there).

- People who exercised lived longer; 15 to 45 minutes daily minutes was best, and beat out 3 hours of sporadic exercise.

- Nonphysical activities, such as book clubs, socializing with friends, board games and other social activities increased longevity by every hour spent.

- Vitamins DID NOT make a difference.

- Moderate caffeine intake (1 to 3 cups of coffee daily) aided longevity.

- Moderate alcohol consumption (2 drinks a day) led to a 10-15 percent reduced risk of death.

- People overweight or of average weight both outlived people who were underweight.

- Risk of dementia doubles every 5 years after age 65.

A few of the findings of the study surprised me. For example, having high blood pressure in your 90s *reduces* your chance of having dementia. I know. I had always imagined that hypertension was always bad, all the time. Also, being a bit overweight, or at least average weight, leads to longer life. Who knew?

MORE ABOUT DEMENTIA

The brain is described by the American Academy of Neurology as a "vascular organ." That just means that it works well when the blood vessels that carry blood to and from it are healthy and unclogged. Clog the arteries and you damage the brain. It's as simple as that. We think with neurons.

If they don't get the oxygen and glucose they need, we start losing brain function. Forgetting where you put your car keys is one thing. Forgetting what they are for is an entirely different matter.

> "If increases in life expectancy continue, more than half of all children born today in developed countries can expect to celebrate their 100th birthday."

The idea that dementia is somehow an inevitable part of aging is bogus, Dr. Kawas says. In an October, 2014 speech at the UC Irvine Institute for Memory Impairments and Neurological Disorders, she told about the Guinness Book of World Records' oldest documented living human, Madame Jeanne-Louis Calmet of Arles, France. She lived to be 122 years old (1875-1997). She rode her bicycle every day until she was 100. She walked every day until she was 115. She NEVER had dementia. That is not just the opinion of her friends and neighbors. Naturally, her longevity attracted the attention of scientists who studied her cognitive functions until she died. She may not have been as alert as a teenager at the time of her death, but, according to Dr. Kawas, she always knew who she was and where she was, and all the important things she needed to know as long as she lived.

Just to be clear, dementia can happen at all ages. People get dementia in their 30s and 40s. It is a disease that costs more than heart disease and cancer combined, says Dr. Kawas. The longer you live, of course, the greater the risk of dementia. But that risk can be lowered significantly by lifestyle choices we make as we age, says Dr. Kawas. (*Source: www.mind.uci.edu/research/90plus-study/#sthash. jm7HU7Rt.dpuf*)

CENTENARIAN "TIDAL WAVE"

Dr. Kawas calls the increase in life expectancy a "tidal wave."

"To give you an idea of the size of that tidal wave," said Dr. Kawas, "I thought this was an amazing quote that I saw a few years ago: 'If increases in life expectancy continue, more than half of all children born today in developed countries can expect to celebrate their 100th birthday." (*Source: Christensen, Aging Populations: The Challenges Ahead, Lancet, 2009*)

Imagine that!

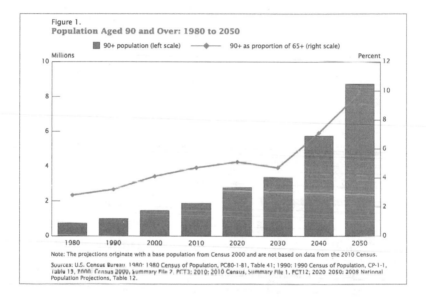

Figure 1.
Population Aged 90 and Over: 1980 to 2050

Note: The projections originate with a base population from Census 2000 and are not based on data from the 2010 Census.

Sources: U.S. Census Bureau, 1980: 1980 Census of Population, PC80-1-B1, Table 41; 1990: 1990 Census of Population, CP-1-1, Table 13; 2000: Census 2000, Summary File 2, PCT3; 2010: 2010 Census, Summary File 1, PCT12; 2020-2050: 2008 National Population Projections, Table 12.

IS IT GENETICS?

The quest to understand why some people live to be 100 and beyond has prompted scientists and doctors to spend countless hours studying the phenomenon. The New England Centenarian Study founded in 1995 is probably the largest. Their most recent research, as this book is written, seems to point to genetics as a key factor in living to the century mark and beyond. According to Dr. Howard

LeWine, chief medical editor for Harvard Health Publications, when researchers analyzed and deciphered the entire genetic codes of a man and a woman who lived past the age of 114, they found a *possible* explanation in their DNA, but they stop short of saying that explains extended lifespans.

Dr. LeWine maintains that "during the first 75 years of life, genes have a relatively small influence on longevity, accounting for only 20 to 25 percent of the reasons that you make it to that age." He says living a longer life has more to do with "not smoking, eating healthfully, getting plenty of exercise, and limiting alcohol."

"Once you hit your mid-80s, genes matter more and more," Dr. LeWine says. "And once your reach your 90s, how much longer you are likely to live was largely determined the day your father's sperm fertilized your mother's egg."

His "top 10 list" of things to do to live longer are:

1. Don't smoke.
2. Be physically active every day.
3. Eat a healthy diet rich in whole grains, lean protein, vegetables and fruits. Reduce or avoid unhealthy saturated fats and trans fats. Instead, use healthier monounsaturated and polyunsaturated fats.
4. Be sure to get enough vitamin D and calcium.
5. Maintain a healthy weight and body shape.
6. Challenge your mind.
7. Build a strong social network.
8. Protect your sight, hearing and general health by following preventive care guidelines.

9. Floss, brush and see a dentist regularly. Poor oral health may have many effects. It can lead to poor nutrition, pain and possibly even a higher risk of heart disease and stroke.

10. Discuss with your doctor whether you need any medicine to help you stay healthy. These might include medicines to control high blood pressure, treat osteoporosis or lower cholesterol, for example. (*Source: www.health.harvard.edu/blog/living-to-100-and-beyond-the-right-genes-plus-a-healthy-lifestyle-201201114092*)

THE NUN STUDY

What role do emotions play in living a longer, healthier life? Quite a large one according to what has been dubbed "The Nun Study," one of the most intriguing experiments to try to determine who gets Alzheimer's disease, who doesn't and why. Having a positive outlook on life and being stable emotionally apparently helps you live longer.

It is called "The Nun Study" because researchers analyzed the lives of 678 elderly Catholic nuns over a 15-year span, starting with essays they had written when they were in their 20s. They scoured the words to determine their emotional health. They gave them cognition tests involving flashcards that required them to name as many animals as they could in one minute. They gave them coins to count and tested them for accuracy and speed. As the nuns died, they studied their brain tissue.

Why nuns? Because they all led similar lives. They were nonsmokers, drank little alcohol and did not have pregnancy-related physical changes. Most of them were teachers in Catholic schools and ate the same food in convent cafeterias.

So what did they find?

- Those who expressed more positive emotions lived much longer (sometimes as many as 10 years longer) than those whose expressions were less positive.
- The better their language skills, the lower their risk of Alzheimer's. The ones whose sentences were brimming with ideas seemed more immune to dementia.
- Nuns who stayed active both physically and mentally lived longer and remained clear-headed.
- Depression increased the risk of cardiovascular disease.
- Those whose personality tests rated them as optimists lived longer lives.

A *New York Times* article, "Nuns Offer Clues to Alzheimer's and Aging," by Pam Belluck, related the story of Sister Esther Boor, "who at 106 speeds through the labyrinth of halls with a royal blue walker, glazes ceramic nativity scenes for the gift shop, and pedals an exercise bike every day, her black veil flapping, an orange towel draped over her legs for modesty.

"'Sometimes I feel like I'm 150, but I just made up my mind I'm not going to give up,' said Sister Esther, who gives her exercise therapists yellow notes with phrases from books she reads. 'Think no evil, do no evil, hear no evil,' she wrote recently, 'and you will never write a best-selling novel.'"

The *Times* article said, "Sister Esther's autobiographical essay, written 80 years ago, is similarly upbeat, speaking fondly of her family and her decision to become a nun." (*Source: www.nytimes.com/2001/05/07/us/nuns-offer-clues-to-alzheimer-s-and-aging.html*)

CHAPTER III

PLANNING FOR LONGEVITY – MAKING YOUR MONEY LAST AS LONG AS YOU DO

"Age is a case of mind over matter.
If you don't mind, it doesn't matter."
    – Satchel Paige

I OFTEN TELL EVERYONE that I'm the luckiest person in the world because I have been blessed with life experiences that allowed me the privilege of being around and learning from the wisdom of the senior generation.

Having been a caregiver for over 30 years of my life, I could navigate family members and friends through the most vulnerable life stages. I've seen the good, the bad and the ugly. I am blessed to have real-life lessons, and to have gleaned from them the wisdom most folks only read about.

I interviewed a surgeon once and asked her how many lives she thought she might have saved in her career. She laughed and said she had never thought about it.

"I just find the problem and do my best—using all my skills, experience and education—to solve it," she said.

"Do any of your patients ever thank you for saving their lives?" I asked.

"Yes, they do," she replied. "And it always catches me a little off-guard when they do. I don't expect that. I was just doing my job."

I thought that to be a beautiful and selfless way to view the professional role we play in life. I often think of where some of my family members would have been had I not cared for them both physically and financially in their later stages of life. Would they have lived in poverty? Become wards of the state? What would their quality of life have been?

In the last 10 years, my professional career has been devoted to helping clients and their families arrange their finances to live out their retirement years without the fear of running out of assets to sustain them. Like that surgeon, when I occasionally receive commendation for my work, I reflect on the fact that I was merely doing what I was put here to do.

WHY PLAN FOR THE LONG HAUL?

So, why plan for the long haul? Because you deserve only the best life has to offer, whether you're 80, 90, 100 or beyond. To borrow a line from my second book, *Retirement Done Right,* you must believe that for the number of years God allows you to walk the earth, He wants you to do so with dignity, prosperity and self-respect.

So, let's assume you are going to live beyond 100. What should you be thinking about?

Typically, in your 60s, you plan for your retirement as though you are going be in it for around 20 to 25 years. You tend to allocate your resources accordingly. Most people go about with a false sense of security that their fixed incomes, such as their Social Security check, will take care of them in their very senior years. They falsely assume they will be less active. As you read some of the true-life experiences of some of the people you will meet in the pages of this book, you will see why I label that a false assumption.

When I question my clients about how much money they think they will need in their golden years, they consistently tell me they think they will need more in their early years of retirement. To their way of thinking, they will spend much less in their upper 70s and early 80s. Sorry to disagree, but that mental model is an archaic one. It is totally wrong.

The information I have gathered in the many interviews of the 90-plus generation I have conducted for this book tells a vastly different story. My research confirms that living longer means a more *active* lifestyle for *longer* periods of time. More travel. More golfing. More fishing.

More of whatever you do that keeps you going.

What's that? Never thought you would be driving at age 94, much less buying a car? Think again! You thought living independently would not figure into your plans past age 85? Think again!

Add to that the cost of funding quality living standards and proper health care, not to mention taxes and inflation, and there is ample evidence that your need for a consistent, permanent income stream will not diminish as you age. So, unlike our parents' generation, we can anticipate many factors that require planning for a long life.

WHAT WOULD YOU HAVE DONE DIFFERENTLY?

New York Yankees baseball great Mickey Mantle is famous for the quip: "If I knew I was going to live this long, I'd have taken better care of myself."

In some of the interviews that follow in this book, I ask the poignant question to some who are well into their 90s, "What would you have done differently in your earlier

years if you knew you would still be this active at this age?"
Most of their responses:

- Saved more

- Worked longer

- Planned better and earlier

- Found something else to do part-time

- Pursued a second career

Did you notice how most of those answers were
financial?

So how do you plan financially for longevity? Pretty
simple. YOU PLAN!

Create a lifestyle plan that takes into consideration living beyond 100. And, if you get it wrong, oh well! Then
spend more money in your 90s, or start gifting to your
family. Or, better yet, find some elderly friends and family
members who didn't plan as well as you, and who need
help, and help them to have a quality of life that they otherwise would not have had.

There are four areas that need to be considered and
pulled together which should lay a foundation for longevity:

Legal planning: Legal documents consider such
contingencies as pre-need guardians. They should be
updated for the various life stages, and should include
asset protection should you need long-term care.

Financial planning: Are your assets positioned to
last a long lifetime? How much risk do you really
need to be taking in your early years of retirement?
What risk is appropriate for what age?

Healthcare planning: How will you fund special healthcare needs, such as long-term care, home health care services, or assisted living?

Lifestyle planning: Where do you plan to spend your golden years? Creating plans to age in place in your home, for example, requires planning. You may need to make modifications to the structure. Do you plan to relocate to a life-care community? That, too, requires advance thought and planning.

Wheel of Life

I will never forget a sign I saw on the wall of an office supply store. In the frame were three words: ALWAYS PLAN AHEAD. But the way the sign had been printed, it was obvious that the one making the letters had not done just that. The words, "ALWAYS" and "PLAN" were too big, and the word, "AHEAD" trailed off into tiny type. Don't become a victim of poor planning. If you don't plan to live a long, active life, you are making a choice to expect an unpredictable outcome. Do you think it's fair that you should be worried about money when you are 95 years old? I don't, either. A common theme I have heard in the interviews I have conducted with seniors, and one I consistently hear from my clients, is the fear of running out of money. Planning is the only discipline that removes the fear. You want to be celebrating your 100th birthday with joy and a passion for life. You want to approach that milestone with a fearless pursuit of your interests and dreams.

The burning question for our age is, "How do you make your money last as long as you do?" It's pretty simple. It may not be easy according to the men and women who allowed me into their lives, but it is simple. The most evident way to make sure your money lasts as long as you do is to STAY HEALTHY. This isn't my advice; it's the wisdom of the many individuals I have talked to in doing the research for this book. They say anyone can live longer, but you have to work at it to live BETTER. That's the real challenge.

Thanks to medical and scientific advances that even a generation ago would have sounded like a good sci-fi movie, our lives will be longer. Americans born today have significantly longer life spans than those born in the 1920s or 1930s. The fastest-growing population segment in the United States today is the 90-plus folks. So, holding onto your health is the key to holding onto your wealth.

Catholic philosopher A.J. Reb Materi is credited with the following famous quote: "Most people spend their health getting their wealth, then they have to spend their wealth to regain their health." This is *not* what you want to do. The idea of a long life does not have to trigger anxiety in anyone. It's the simple things you do that help you journey through the most senior stages of your life. Here are some insights I gathered on simple strategies:

- Eat healthy.
- Drink wine.
- Don't give into pain—work through it.
- Keep your mind active by reading, doing what you love doing, and socializing.
- Stay alive in your faith.
- Focus on your family.
- Rise above your adversity—don't focus on problems.
- Volunteer and keep serving others.
- Focus on others and not on yourself.
- Have a purpose.
- Find something you enjoy and do it for a long time.

These simple tips are directly from the wisdom of the more mature Americans.

The challenge we face today is converting a world built by and for younger people into a world that supports and engages populations that are living to 100 and beyond. I had a real-life experience with this.

I have always been health-conscious, especially since my cancer diagnosis a few years ago—well, to be exact, over 28 years ago as I write this. I always carefully considered what I put in my body. I eat simply and healthy. I am physically active. When I reached my upper 50s and early 60s, I noticed that the trainers at the gym I use were not altering exercise routines for me as I moved along in years. The average age of the trainers I was using was 25 years old. They geared their workouts for younger patrons. One day, when I was working out at the gym, it occurred to me that they had no idea how to help women my age achieve their fitness goals. Their routines were much too strenuous and rough. And, more importantly, they did not focus on the physical importance of flexibility, balance and core strength. I kept getting hurt and I didn't understand why. Then I got the right trainer, for me, anyway. This professional turned out to be a 52-year-old Olympic athlete who understood the human body, and how to coax muscles over the age of 50 into maintaining their strength and elasticity *without injury*. I learned a valuable physical fitness lesson— focusing on the same exercise routines that I used when I was in my 30s and 40s can be a recipe for pain and disaster in my 50s and 60s.

As we age, the need shifts from endurance to core strength. We need to maintain flexibility and balance along with strength. The bottom line to keep us "older folk" from falling and breaking bones and such is to spend more time with less exertion and stress to the bones and muscles. After two years of working out with the right type of trainer, I see the value of working with an "age appropriate" professional—someone who is interested in helping you continue to keep totally fit and in great health, and who knows what that might mean for you, even if you are no longer a teenager.

In addition to remaining physically healthy, holding onto your mental and emotional *health* is also the key to holding onto your *wealth*. What I found amazing about the individuals I interviewed, as well as the secrets of the centenarians and super-centenarians we read about daily, is just how crucial mental and emotional health is to living a long life without running out of money.

It was also made abundantly clear to me in the interviews that I conducted how essential it is to have a purposeful life. None of the sparkling personalities you will read about here believed in wallowing in self-pity, because they were no longer teenagers. They identified themselves with their capacity to contribute to society at whatever age they were. None of them gave any evidence of focusing on their aches and pains. They looked forward each day to interacting with others. They saw their glasses as half full instead of half empty, even if their glass was a quarter full.

CHAPTER IV

LEAVING A STORY TO BE TOLD THROUGH THE AGES–LEGACY PLANNING REDEFINED

"What we do for ourselves dies with us. What we do for others and the world remains and is immortal."
– Albert Pine

FOR THE PURPOSES OF THIS DISCUSSION, the focus on legacy planning refers to more than the simple act of having your legal documents organized, stating clearly and concisely what you wish to leave behind when you walk out on life. Your legacy is much greater than the money or property you leave behind to your loved ones, or what you bequeath to your favorite charity. It has to do with how you have lived your life, and the story you leave behind for your loved ones, whether they are family members, friends or simply people who have watched you live your life to its fullest. Are you leaving purposeful stories that describe the legacy by which you want to be remembered? You are more than the money you leave behind. You will be remembered for something far greater than that.

36 HOURS TO LIVE

I was in a hospital waiting room. The doctor came in and I knew from the expression on his face that the news was not good. My mother had only 36 hours to live. I would need to call family and friends so they could come and say their goodbyes.

My mother had gone from being the epitome of health to my having to take her to the emergency room because she was having difficulty breathing. At first, I thought it was some kind of emotional anxiety. Perhaps it was a re-action to the news that her best friend and second cousin had just passed away unexpectedly. I would learn that my mother's 86-year-old heart was not strong. The doctor told me she had less than two days to live.

Stunned and shaking, I fumbled in my purse and found a notepad to make a list of everyone I needed to call. After all, I am a list maker and a planner, and why change my personal style at a time of crisis? I knew I couldn't miss anyone who was special to my mother. One by one, I called my sisters, my mother's nieces and neph-ews, and mother's closest friends. I couldn't get to every-one alone, so I used a triage approach, assigning families to my sisters to contact so we could get to the masses. I knew I would spend the next 36 hours sleepless in St. Luke's Hospital in Jacksonville, Florida.

It wasn't long before family members started arriving. Then friends began trickling in. Word had gotten around to others I had not called—to neighbors and others my mother had influenced over the years. Within just a few hours, my family and my mother's friends had taken over the entire hospital waiting room. At one point, I count-ed 80 people. They had filled the waiting room, and an overflow crowd was mingling in the hallway outside. One of the hospital administrators sent word that we would all have to leave. I ignored the request. My mother was dying. These people wanted to be with her as she transitioned to another life and I was not about to dismiss them. She obviously meant a lot to these people, and I wanted to honor my mother's legacy.

A representative of hospital security came. I explained to them that we just needed more space, that's all. They offered me another room, and that seemed to satisfy the hospital administration folks. I was relieved. But as I shuttled from one room to the next, I found myself meeting people I did not know. Where had these people come from? How did they know my mother?

MY MOTHER'S LEGACY

I learned a great deal about my mother from this experience. She was not an educated woman, nor was she endowed with great wealth and power. She was ordinary by all the common standards one might apply. But it seemed that she was deeply loved by all these people. I spoke to as many of them as I could make my way to in the next few hours, and as I did so, I heard story after story of how my mother had personally impacted their lives. Some told me of the good times they had shared with her. Others told me of how, when they were having problems, my mother had been there for them, listening patiently with true, genuine concern.

I was overwhelmed with pride and appreciation for her. I was also—surprised is not the word—stunned to learn the way she had touched so many. Her physical condition prevented her from going anywhere. She had been homebound for years. But she refused to let that stop her from serving others, or from reaching out to stay connected with her family and friends.

The telephone was my mother's power tool. Even though she had two bad knees with bone-on-bone arthritis, and each step she took caused her intense pain, she refused to sit around and mope all day. Here is a sampling of what people in that waiting room told me:

"She called me every week to see how I was doing and how my family was. She never missed a single week checking on us."

"She always sent me a plate of food anytime she cooked my favorite meal."

"When my grandson was baptized, or when my husband had surgery, or when anything happened to us, she always called to check on us, or congratulate us. She never forgot us."

"She had a heart so big for the community, and she can never be replaced."

"She sent us our favorite cookies every Christmas since our mother died—she never forgot about us".

"Whenever we dropped by for a brief visit, she always made us Arabic coffee and offered us some of her homemade cookies; and we never left without taking cookies home."

My mother, an immigrant who didn't drive and spoke halting English as a second language, had used her heart, her spirit and soul to reach out to those around her. God had given her the simple gifts of a spirit of hospitality and an unconditional love for others. She was living her purpose, and I didn't even realize it.

Standing there in that hospital waiting room, listening to the stories of her visitors, it occurred to me that the mother I thought I knew was not the person that others saw. I knew a tough woman who cared for her family like they were her sole responsibility. I knew a devout woman who prayed unceasingly for those closest to her. But I really had no idea of the extent of her goodness. Her understanding of family went far beyond the traditional definition of the word. She had obviously adopted many people who were not her blood relation into her inner circle. I reflected on the fact that, when we had service people working around our home, either inside or out, she would invite them in for a meal. She treated everyone like family and they remembered her for it.

I prayed to God that he would let her live a little while longer, just so I could learn more from this woman I thought I knew so well. Knowing her through the eyes of these individuals whose lives she had touched was an epiphany for me. She had begun writing her legacy the day she was born. Early on, she had known what her God-given purpose was—to serve others regardless of where she was in life's journey.

A LIFE EXTENSION

My mother's 36-hour time limit came and went, and she was still alive. The cardiologist told me that she was being discharged from the hospital, but not to get my hopes up.

"She is 86 years old," the doctor said. "She has lived a good, long life." I turned to Dr. Graciela (Grace) Diez-Hoeck, a good friend and neighbor, who was also my mother's internal medicine doctor and asked for her advice.

"We just need to put her on a dopamine drip to keep her comfortable through this night," Grace said. "If she lives through the night, we will re-group with the cardiologist in the morning."

The cardiologist was shocked to learn that my mother was still alive the next morning. So much for modern medical science. Not only was she alive, she was alert and talking! Grace's gift as a caring physician, with the prayers offered up for my mother, coupled with my mother's fighting spirit, changed everything!

The cardiologist told me that what my mother needed was an aortic valve replacement and quadruple bypass surgery, but it was too risky at her age, and he would not perform the operation. I pushed back. I knew my mother's fighting spirit. I knew that life and death are in the hands of God, not attending physicians.

Since my mother was quite alert, and able to talk to us now, I asked her what she wanted to do. I made her fully aware of the risks. I told her that there was a good chance she could die on the operating table. She was quite clear and candid about her choice. She wanted to have the surgery. From her way of looking at things, if God wanted her to live, she would live. It was in His hands. If it was her time, then so be it. That was her thinking. She felt like she had seen her entire family, and she was OK dying if that was to be the case. It was settled then. She would have her surgery.

I prayed more earnestly than I can ever remember praying before that she would pull through. There was so much more I could learn from her. I apologized to her for having been so busy with career and caregiving of my own that I had not gotten to know her as I had wanted.

Was I unique in this regard? I don't think so. How many of us don't spend time with the older ones in our family—our parents and grandparents—learning who they are so we can carry their legacy forward to future generations? Then, when they are gone, it is too late.

God honored my prayers. My mother not only survived the operation, but had seven more great years afterward. The doctor who had not expected her to live proclaimed it a miracle. He had said that even if she did make it through the operation, she would be confined to a wheelchair for the rest of her life. That turned out not to be the case, either. She overcame the odds and, after a long rehab period, was able to walk and live independently. They knew her physical being, and were making their diagnosis on that basis. But they didn't know her psyche and her fighting spirit. They had also not considered the power of prayer, and the involvement of a higher power.

Those "extra" seven years with my mother compelled me to put my "busyness" and my career on temporary hold, and focus on some of the more meaningful things of life. Mom and I rekindled the tradition of family holiday gatherings at my home, with the aroma of her cooking (she insisted on cooking) filling the house, and the laughter of her grandchildren and great-grandchildren filling the room. We created projects together. She loved to crochet, and made afghans for each daughter, grandchild and great-grandchild, even making several extra afghans for great-grandchildren yet to be born. This was part of her special legacy. Now, when a new great-grandchild of hers comes into the world, I take great pride in giving one of these to this new member of the family. Someday, when the child is old enough, they will know that it came from her and, in that way, they will also get to know her in some small way.

Why am I sharing all of this with you? I believe we all have a legacy to pass along to those who come after us. It's a part of who we are that we transfer to others before we "shuffle off this mortal coil." That legacy has more to do with who we are than what we possess. Of all my mother's five daughters, I believe I was the luckiest. I finally got to understand the true meaning of legacy before it was too late. I confess that I had come to view my caregiving responsibilities as a taxing and oftentimes overwhelming burden. I was convinced that, for some celestial reason I could not comprehend, I had been appointed to bear the responsibility of looking after others with little time for myself. What I had learned from my mother in the last few years of her life was that it was not a burden at all, but a blessed privilege. The legacy my mother left is a life well-lived through service to others. Was that why God allowed her to live an extended life? So that I could be re-birthed? I think so.

Mother died Oct. 18, 2006. One of the toughest things I have ever had to do was help my mother transition from this world to the next. Her death gave me life of a different sort from that day forward. I knew from then on that I wanted to leave a legacy that would honor my parents, and provide a good example for my nieces and nephews, and the grandnieces and grandnephews, and great-grand nieces and great-grand nephews to follow.

AN INVITATION

I wish to invite you to do some legacy planning for yourself. Not the typical legacy planning found in wills and trusts. While that type of legacy planning is important, it is temporary; it is used up and then forgotten. What remains and is permanent is the story of yourself you leave behind. That kind of legacy has permanence and definition. It is the type of legacy that gives your family, and society-at-large, a gift that has generational influence and power.

Your legacy could be something as simple as an annual Christmas letter, sent to all of your family, highlighting your family activities. Or it could be a special recipe you make at each family reunion. It could be sleepovers with the grandkids. Or it could be the Saturday morning fishing trips with your youngsters. The football games you attend together or some other athletic activity.

FOUR WAYS TO LEAVE A LEGACY

In doing research for this book, I ran across an article in the "Personal Finance" section of *Forbes'* online magazine, dated Aug. 1, 2013, entitled "4 Smart Ways to Leave a Legacy."

The article, written by Bart Astor, acknowledged that we may not be able to leave a legacy that touches the entire world, but we can touch those around us.

"Your legacy is putting your stamp on the future," Astor writes. "It is a way to make some meaning of your existence: 'Yes, world of the future, I was here. Here is my contribution. Here's why I hope my life mattered.'"

The article identified four simple ways to leave a legacy. I am confident you can add many more ways of your own. Here are Astor's ideas:

Provide a family history: "Researching your genealogy is a wonderful way to let your kids and grandkids understand where you and they came from." Astor points readers to websites like Ancestry.com and Archives.gov where you can build a family tree. He invites readers to add a personal touch by describing your relationship with your parents and grandparents, aunts, uncles, siblings and children.

I suggest you list everything you know about them—even including details that may be less than savory. If you don't do it, it may be lost to history. I can think of no better way to make these ancestors live to the younger generation who reads about them in your family tree "diary."

Give to charity: "Another way to leave a legacy is by contributing money or the equivalent to a charitable cause that reflects your values," suggests Astor. "You could create a meaningful gifting plan so your kids and grandkids will receive money while you're alive, allowing you to watch them benefit from your generosity."

Astor suggests that wealthier individuals could even create "a charitable foundation or a trust that provides on-going distributions, so the gift has more lasting value." He gives the example of a scholarship endowment to the giver's alma mater that would benefit future students, or an annuity with the university as the beneficiary. That's a cool idea because it pays interest to the givers during their lifetime, but goes to the charity upon their death, plus they may get a tax credit for some of the donation.

My special friend and client, Pat, who wanted to leave a legacy but had no children, no siblings or anyone else, loved supporting poor, hungry children. So, during her lifetime, we created a charitable foundation to gift to her favorite charities that support her values. Now, I have the privilege of continuing to honor her life well beyond her exit out of this earth by gifting to entities that honor her passion for helping poor, underprivileged children. Her legacy will carry on by building orphanages in third world countries so girls can have a home and a hope for the future. Charitable gifting goes on well beyond our temporary life on earth.

Write a legacy letter: "Think about everything you'd want to tell your loved ones and your survivors if you knew you didn't have long to live, then put it all in a letter to them," suggests Astor.

We encourage our clients to add this to a section we put in their family estate book. The section is called "Instructions to Heirs," and it's a beautiful thing to leave them. It's more than just mechanical instructions; it's about the heartfelt things you want to say to them that you may not have ever said. No surprises here, please. You don't want to share with them any of the ugly things in your past that would throw them into an emotional spin. I even suggest writing a letter to your as-yet-unborn grandchildren, telling them who you are and that you love them. They may treasure it one day more than you could ever know.

For me, the legacy letter I got was verbal. I was right there guiding my mother through her last days on earth. I got all the instructions I needed, which pertained to making sure the family stayed together: Take care of your sisters. Don't stay alone. And find someone to share your life with when I'm gone. As you see, none of the instructions in her legacy had anything to do with *things*—only relationships and service to the family.

Prepare an ethical will: "An ethical will is the logical extension of a legacy letter." Astor explains that, centuries ago, elders orally conveyed their values to the next generation. An ethical will allows you to share the meaning of your life, your belief and valuable life lessons with succeeding generations. It isn't a binding document, like a testamentary will, but it is like telling your story. These days, it can easily be digitally recorded on video and could include snapshots from your photo albums.

It reminds me of the movie *The Ultimate Gift*, in which a young man by the name of Jason is heir to his grandfather's fortune. In that beautiful story, the young man is sent on 12 tasks, which his deceased grandfather, Red, calls "gifts." He must complete each of these assignments of discovery before he can lay claim to his inheritance. The point of the movie, and the book by the same name, is not just endowing future generations with money, but teaching them what you have learned about life. (*Source: www. forbes.com/sites/nextavenue/2013/08/01/4-smart-ways-to-leave-a-legacy/2/#4c36fa5a7837*)

FINDING ONE'S PURPOSE

A few years ago, I attended a woman's retreat at my church. The advertised purpose of the retreat was "spiritual renewal." I had no idea what to expect. I'm not sure I knew what the term "spiritual renewal" meant. Was I going to commune with God in some special way that I had not communed before? Would this event help me through some of the challenges I was facing at the time? The retreat came right after my mother had passed away, and I was struggling to figure out the next step, now that my caregiving for her had ended. I was also not finding fulfillment in my career at the time. If life was a book, I had no idea what the next chapter of mine was to be.

When we registered for the event, we were asked to give the names of two close relatives or friends who would serve as emergency contacts. At the time, I wondered what activities were in store for me that would necessitate an emergency contact, but I put down the names of two family members. But it was a ruse! What none of us knew was that the organizers of the event would contact these individuals and obtain from them and others letters expressing how we had influenced their lives. They would then share these letters with participants in the retreat.

I was blown away when I heard what kind and wonderful things my family members had to say about me that they had never said to me. Their sentiments were more precious than jewels or gold. To think they had those feelings all along, and I was unaware of them.

"Thank you so much for being the rock in our family," wrote my nephew, Jason, and his wife. *"And we don't just mean us; we mean the entire family. We only hope that you will come to us and let us be there for you when you are in need."*

My youngest great-niece wrote, *"You have been an inspiration to me in so many ways. You sacrificed so many things for Grandma to live with you; to me, you are selfless. You care so much about others, always putting yourself last. You are strong and independent and those characteristics are rare. You are an amazing woman with a huge heart. I will always look up to you because of what you sacrificed for your loved ones and the fact that you are extremely wise with so much to teach. You and my mom are such role models for me. I think the two of you leave some daunting shoes to fill. I love the fact that I come from strong women who have shown me that it is courage, strength, faith in the Lord, and love that is the recipe for a successful life. Thank you, Aunt Jeannette, for being who you are and loving us so much. We love you with all our hearts. God will bless you forever!"*

And that is just a sampling. My eyes were wet and my heart was full.

When my mother was on her "death bed," I heard what she had meant to those in her circle. Now I knew that I must continue to mirror that same spirit of self-sacrifice and caring for others, and carry on her legacy. Two days before she actually passed away, Mother told me she wanted me to "take care of the family and keep them together." Fueled by this outpouring of appreciation and love, wild horses couldn't keep me from following through on her wishes.

The point is this: If you feel such sentiments toward loved ones, by all means share it with them while you both are still alive. You never know what good it will do. A life well-lived is words put to action, and evidenced by those whose lives you influenced. What will your legacy to the world be?

CHAPTER V

WISDOM OF THE
AGES INTERVIEWS

WHO DOESN'T WANT TO LIVE a long and fulfilling life? What exactly is the secret of doing so? Is getting to that three-digit age just in the genes, and therefore something we can't predict or control? Or is there some common denominator that will get us there? I have interviewed several people who have been blessed with good health and many years and asked them for their stories and they have graciously given me much wisdom. Every story is different. Each life experience, as you would expect, is unique.

Most of the people you will meet here were still living by the time this book went to press in late 2016. Unfortunately, some of them have passed on. I say unfortunately because the treasure lost is ours. Most of those who have passed on would not have us mourn their passing, but would have us rejoice that we could make their acquaintance.

But as you read their stories, you may find a common thread. I know I did in many of them. These wonderful people opened the doors of their hearts for me and allowed me to peek inside their minds and share their thoughts with you, dear reader. I hope you learn a lot from what they had to say. I know I did.

DR. FRANCES BARTLETT KINNE, 98

There is no doubt that Dr. Frances Bartlett Kinne (pro-nounced like "skinny" without the "s"), at age 98, is an impressive woman. Talk about legacy—her list of accomplishments and awards could fill the rest of this book. But what impressed me the most was her cheerfulness, her smile and her approachability.

"Please call me Fran," she said, instantly putting me at ease. In a few minutes, it felt as if we had been old friends for years.

She is a woman of many firsts:

First woman to serve as dean of a fine arts college in the United States. First woman to serve as president of a Florida university (Jacksonville University). At least six public facilities that I know of are named in her honor. I interviewed her for this book shortly after she had delivered the keynote address to graduates of Jacksonville University, Dec. 12, 2015, where she is believed to be the oldest-known person to deliver a commencement speech to a graduating class at a masters-level university.

Dr. Frances Bartlett Kinne

"I didn't used to talk about my age—until I hit 90," she told reporters for *The Wave*, a campus newspaper. "Now I think it's an inspiration to others to see how much can be achieved in life."

Fran was JU's president for 10 years, was chancellor from 1989 to 1994, and has served as chancellor emeritus since 1994. She began her JU career in 1958 as a humanities professor, and was selected as founding dean of JU's College of Fine Arts in 1961. She served in that capacity until being named JU's president in 1979. Under her leadership, the college established what is now the Davis College of Business, the School of Nursing, the Aviation program, and the College of Arts and Sciences, among others.

Fran's mother was a librarian and her father was a newspaper publisher. A music lover, she still plays the piano and at one time conducted a school orchestra. She is an Iowa native and graduate of Drake University with degrees in music education, and earned a doctorate from the University of Frankfurt in Germany.

One of Fran's favorite expressions and one she uses to inspire others is: "Go out and make the world a better place."

"I went to Germany shortly after World War II to enroll in the University of Frankfurt," remembered Fran, "and I didn't feel very welcome. I went home in tears one night because I was trying to register at the university and the other registrants kept pushing me out of line. I went home and told my husband what had happened, and he explained what was going on. He told me that Americans had bombed their city and nearly destroyed Frankfurt in one night. After that, I went back with an entirely different feeling. I dressed differently to blend in. I had a Buick sports car. I parked it two blocks away. In my philosophy class, we didn't have enough chairs, so I sat on the floor. It took about a year, but they finally accepted me and we got along fine after that."

She was on the staff of Gen. Douglas MacArthur in Japan in the postwar era of the 1940s. "We really weren't supposed to associate with the local people, but I did anyway, because my heart went out to them," said Fran. "In fact, I got permission from General MacArthur to help in their schools, most of which had been burned or bombed to pieces. I managed to get 275 Americans over there to go and help. It was very rewarding, but at the same time frustrating that I couldn't do more to help those people." When asked what was the secret of her longevity and seemingly boundless energy at nearly 100, she replied: "I'm a positive thinker. ... I teach it. I talk about it all the time."

"The way you handle difficulty makes all the difference in the world," she advised. "Don't gripe. Don't wake up griping. If you are around negative people, it will rub off on you. If you are a positive thinker, you will live at least 10 years longer."

"It is important to keep the body healthy," she said, "but I also say it's what's in our minds. I'm always looking forward. The people I see the most are 18- to 25-year-olds. They keep me thinking young, believe me."

At Christmastime, Fran says she receives around 2,000 Christmas cards from all over the world. Many of them come from the more than 16,000 students whose lives she has touched in one way or another. She says the education she has received through her involvement with other people is of far greater value to her than all of the many degrees she has earned at colleges and universities.

Dr. Kinne with Bob Hope and Jack Benny

Fran is listed in more than 25 *Who's Who* and similar publications, as well as *Two Thousand Women of Achievement, Community Leaders in America, Notable Americans,* the *Directory of American Scholars,* and *Personalities of the South.* She was also the first female President of the Jacksonville Rotary Club, and was inducted by former Florida Gov. Bob Graham into the Florida Women's Hall of Fame. In 2015, she was awarded the Lifetime Achievement Award at the 12th Annual Women of Influence Awards in Jacksonville.

She has also been responsible for bringing many famous people to Jacksonville. The list includes President Gerald Ford, Winston Churchill, the Rev. Billy Graham, Linus Pauling, Charlton Heston, and maestro Arthur Fiedler (17 times). She even brought Bob Hope, who was a close friend of hers, and Jack Benny together for an appearance at the JU campus. She said she and Bob Hope became friends while entertaining troops. "He taught me how to dress fast and organize closets by color."

When I asked Fran what advice she would give some-one who was planning to retire, her eyes twinkled and she responded in a flash, "Don't retire!"

She said that her parents made her give gifts to others when she was 5 years old, a precious legacy which she says taught her to be selfless, always giving.

"Do a favor for someone else; it will change your attitude," she said. "Everyone has a different DNA. It was a gift from God. Find your DNA—your gift—and give it back to the world."

Quoting Albert Einstein, she said, "There are two ways to go through life—thinking that nothing is a miracle, or everything is a miracle. I choose to think that *everything* is a miracle."

Fran said her mother lived to be 101 years old and never stopped wearing high heels until she tripped and broke her hip and "the doctor made her give them away."

"When you keep this alive," laughed Fran, pointing to her head, "you are able to do many things, even when you are older. But life isn't about me, it's about others. You will find when you move into that vast area of serving others, that it will energize you and make you happy. It makes all the difference in the world."

BUGS BOWER, 93

His real name is Maurice, but he is known the world over as Bugs Bower, a nickname his World War II 89th Infantry buddies hung on him because, like the witty, mischievous rabbit of Warner Brothers cartoon fame, he was always moving, always thinking of things to do.

Bugs Bower

Bugs is probably most famous for his accomplishments in the music field. His name is synonymous with the word "hit." He is the recipient of two Grammy awards and nine "Gold Record Million Seller" awards, and has produced, composed and arranged hundreds of recordings. The list of famous musicians and musical groups he has worked with includes Perry Como, Cab Calloway, Bing Crosby, Kool & The Gang, Steve Allen, Brian Hyland, Bobby Rydell, Joe Pesci, Captain Kangaroo, Sammy Kaye, Liza Minnelli and Charlie Barnet, among many others.

Better-known as Dr. Bower now (he is a professor of music), he works and lives in both Ponte Vedra, Florida, and South Hampton, New York, owning two identical homes in each location. He summers in New York and winters in sunny Florida. An accomplished musician, he went to New York's famed Juilliard School of Music at age 20 and has been teaching others the joy of music ever since.

"I still play every day, just to keep my fingers going," he said. "I believe that people who play and listen to music live longer and happier lives." Bugs has authored several best-selling books, all related to music, including "Bop," "Bop Duets," "Chords and Progressions" and "Rhythms," as well as several children's music books and CDs.

Born July 16, 1922, in Atlantic City, Bugs grew up near the piers where his father, Fred, played in bands and arranged music. Atlantic City was famous at the time for beauty pageants. Fred Bower wrote and arranged music for these contests. He was 101 years old when he died.

There was music all summer long in Atlantic City—in the big ballrooms, on Million Dollar Pier and Steel Pier. As a kid, Bugs rode his bicycle around town, whistling tunes as he went. Soon, he tried his hand at the trumpet and picked it up virtually overnight. When he heard Glenn Miller's band and the swing music that was popular in the '30s, he knew what he wanted to do. By age 17, he was earning $1 an hour playing trumpet in swing bands. Shortly thereafter, he moved to New York City, "where the action was."

"I got a room for $9 a night," Bugs recalled. "The only problem was I had to share it with two other guys who snored, and it was right next to a noisy elevated train track. It wasn't very glamorous."

While he was in the Big Apple, World War II exploded on the world scene and Bugs enlisted in the Army, taking his trumpet with him.

"As soon as I heard Harry James play the trumpet, I wanted to be like him," says Bugs. "I didn't learn to play the piano until later in life."

Courtesy of Uncle Sam, Bugs entered the prestigious Juilliard School of Music where he met people who would dramatically influence his music career.

The "Home/News" section of *The Florida Times Union* ran a feature article on Bugs in its issue of Oct. 29, 2015. The article, written by Matt Soergel, told of his experiences as a soldier/musician in World War II.

Sgt. Bugs Bower led an Army dance band in Europe during World War II. They'd play for the troops, and he saw many a war-weary fighting man cry when he heard real American music.

"He knew right off that playing in a dance band meant he stood a lot better chance than most guys of not dying. Yet, playing in a dance band didn't keep him from seeing things that would give you nightmares, like the dead bodies—hundreds, if not thousands of dead bodies—at a Nazi concentration camp called Ohrdruf, dead people left behind after the 89th overran the camp.

"A film crew just spent four hours interviewing him about that, and told him he'll soon be able to see the footage at the United States Holocaust Memorial Museum in Washington, D.C. Standing by his garage after telling a lot of stories, near the American flag he flies every day, Bugs says he knows he should go to the museum to see himself there.

"'But why do I got to go see that? Hell, I'd rather see blondes.

An Itsy Bitsy Bikini

"After the war, Bugs played trumpet for the Ice Capades in Atlantic City, then went to Juilliard School of Music. Trouble was, the teachers played classical music and he was be-bop. He left, and began teaching music. Then at the suggestion of his mentor, trumpeter Charles Colin, he wrote an instruction manual for aspiring jazz cats called Bop, by 'Bugs' Bowers.

"That was a hit, so he wrote a whole series of instruction books that still sell today.

"He was also arranging songs, which led to working for bandleader Sammy Kaye—an early step on a long career producing and arranging music, hiring musicians, promoting records, dreaming up new records, and even writing songs.

"Writing a song? No problem. Give him five minutes, Bugs says, and he can come up with a tune.

"He was usually behind the scenes like that, as when he worked with a promising 15-year-old singer named Brian Hyland, who in 1960 was given a sure-fire hit to record: 'Itsy Bitsy Teenie Weenie Yellow Polka Dot Bikini.' Bugs—labeled by a newspaper report at the time as Hyland's 'mentor'says he arranged the song and hired the musicians and backup singers.

"The 'Bikini' single needed a B-side, so Bugs and his friend Earl Shuman came up with one: 'Don't Dilly Dally Sally,' a catchy number in its own right."

In our interview with Bugs Bower, we learned many things about this nonagenarian that you wouldn't know unless you asked. For example:

- He pays his bills immediately.
- He goes to church and thanks God daily for his blessed life.
- He takes no medications because he is never sick.
- He feels no stress because when a problem comes along, he solves it if he can and, if he can't, he refuses to worry about it.
- He is a positive thinker and refuses to wallow in negativism of any sort.

- He goes to sleep thinking about music and playing music in his head, and wakes up with music on his mind.

Bugs's success in the music business was a combination of talent, perseverance and good timing, he admits.

"In 1949, I was writing music for the Charlie Barnet Band, and Charlie told me I should write a music book," recounts Bugs. "So I wrote *Bop* and sent the book to music stores across the country. My army buddies were spread across the country, and they would send me the yellow page ads of music stores in their towns, and we would send them the book. Little by little, it just took off. That was my first music book. I think it sold for 75 cents. Soon, I was making $100 a week off the book. That was big money in those days."

Walk to the Beat, another million-seller for Bugs, was produced to help people listen to music that would give them a rhythm to keep up a brisk walking pace. It sold so many copies that the royalties paid for one of Bugs's homes.

Bugs created his own breaks in the music business. In the late 1960s, he was having difficulty getting the music he recorded played by the DJs. All he knew was, he wanted a hit record. Major record companies were paying the disc jockeys millions of dollars to play their records, and Bugs just couldn't compete. That's when he found Kool & the Gang, a talented group that played a fusion of jazz, funk and soul, but couldn't read music. It was a good match. Bugs could write music they could follow and was a good promoter. Songs like "Celebration" and "Funky Stuff" soon dominated the air waves and Bugs had his hits. Tobacco-maker RJ Reynolds soon came calling with an idea. Kool was also the spelling of a popular brand of menthol cigarettes. The company offered a contract that would have made millions for Bugs and the band if they would promote the brand.

But the answer was no. Robert "Kool" Bell, whose Muslim name was Muhammad Bayyan, told the tobacco company they neither drank alcohol nor smoked.

Bugs is very patriotic. He is proud to have served as a soldier in World War II and puts out his American flag on his front porch every morning.

"I spent 42 months from 1942 to 1945 fighting in the European theater," he recalls. "The thing I remember the most was trying to keep my feet dry. It seemed like my boots were wet all the time."

Even during the war, music played a major role in his life. "They asked me to pick 40 men and form two orchestras," he said. "We toured the front lines. When the men heard us play the music from back home, it brought tears to their eyes—even the officers cried."

I asked Bugs what he worries about at this point in his life.

"Nothing!" was his quick response. "I have absolutely no stress. I don't believe in stress. I write and sing music in my head instead of mulling over negative stuff. I like to turn off the world and play my piano."

Bugs introduced us to Kathryn, the love of his life, who is 73 years old and had just retired from her full-time job as an adjunct professor of biology at Nassau Community College in Garden City, New York, where she had been a faculty member for 50 years. But, she still teaches classes in the summer when they go to their New York home for the summer. At the time of this writing, they have been together for 36 years and are still having fun, says Bugs. Their favorite things to do are enjoying sunsets together and trying the many restaurants in the Jacksonville and Ponte Vedra area.

I asked Bugs what would be the one piece of advice he would give those approaching retirement.

"Never retire," he said. "Find something you love to do and do it (Bugs is still working, writing music books). And play a musical instrument if you can. That will keep you forever young."

Dr. Quentin Green, 94

If you search for "Quentin Lafayette Green" on Google, you will discover this 94-year-old doctor who still works three days per week, seeing patients and dispensing the wisdom he has collected over nine decades of life. He is writing a book (*The Cosmic Religion*, and owns a cattle ranch in Chuluota, Florida. In addition to being an author, physician and rancher, he is also loved by his family as a caring father and grandfather.

He was born in Michigan and attended grade school at St. James in downtown Orlando, Florida. He began his medical training as a pre-med student at the University of Texas in Austin, working at the Federal Land Bank while going to night school. Then World War II came along, and he was called into service. He joined the navy, and after boot camp in San Diego, California, he became a corpsman at San Diego Naval Hospital. While in the Navy, he survived an attack of polio virus, but was discharged from the Navy with PPS, post-polio syndrome, a condition that still limits him physically to some degree.

Dr. Quentin Green

After graduating from Baylor College of Medicine, Houston, Texas, in 1948, Quentin completed his internship at Jefferson Davis Hospital in Houston. He served a surgical residency at Jefferson Davis and the Veterans' Administration Hospital in Houston from 1950 until 1952. Between 1952 and 1954, he was called back to service for the Korean conflict and served as a U.S. Navy flight surgeon.

According to a biographic in *For Your Lifestyle*, a Center for Nutritional Studies newsletter, Quentin then shipped out to Sangley Point in the Philippines with a Navy aircraft patrol squadron where he also had additional duty in the dependents' clinic, taking care of wives and children of active military service members. It was there, in 1953, that he developed polio.

"At that time, polio patients in the area were transferred to Clark Air Force Base in the Philippines for treatment," he said. "I recovered and returned to work with my squadron and then was transferred back to San Diego. I still had some time left to serve in the military, so the Navy offered me several interesting duty stations. My choice was

Japan and together with my Philippine experience I was exposed to two great cultures during those tours of duty."

He was discharged from the Navy in 1954 as a Lieutenant Commander. He subsequently obtained an interim OB-GYN residency at Queen of Angels Hospital in Los Angeles. This was followed by a three-year OB-GYN residency at Charity Hospital in New Orleans.

Quentin was married during his last year of residency at Charity Hospital. He considered his options on where to practice. Because he had traveled so much, he held licenses in Texas, California, Louisiana, Arizona and Florida. Fortunately for us he decided to come to Florida in 1958 and open up his practice in Orlando. Quentin and his wife had six children, five boys and one girl. Always a progressive thinker and one who embraced technology, he was one of the first to incorporate computers into his practice in 1970.

According to the article in *For Your Lifestyle*, Quentin decided to phase out of obstetrics and continue his surgery and gynecology practice. "I really enjoyed OB. It was a happy part of medicine dealing with pregnant patients," he says. Right before phasing out of OB, he delivered his first set of triplets.

Quentin is active in his community. In 1970, he founded the Drug Abuse Council of Orange County, a drug rehabilitation headquarters for teenagers and their families located in the home formally occupied by the Green family and donated to the council. The Council moved to new headquarters after a fire, but still operates today under the name "Green House" in honor of its founder. He also helped convert a Winter Garden showcase mansion into a Share-A-Home facility for active senior citizens who shared everyday expenses.

The *For Your Lifestyle* bio explained how he became interested in diet and nutrition: "Summers on his grandparents' farm in southern Illinois exposed Dr. Green to a rural lifestyle, which included no electricity, no running water and an outhouse. Their farming business involved corn and hogs. The rural lifestyle gave him a chance to draw comparisons with his city life in Chicago and Houston during the 1930s. It was during this time that he was able to observe farm living first-hand and realize that livestock in the farming communities were better fed nutritionally than the farm families themselves. His mother's vegetarian and health food knowledge paved the way for his interest in diet and nutrition."

When asked to what he attributes his longevity, he said, "Genetics and good health habits."

"When you retire, enjoy it," he said. "I try to do everything I enjoy, only in moderation. Avoid excesses—too many cocktail parties, too much salt. I still run my ranch—well, my daughter and I—and I still see patients. I enjoy my work very much."

Big Oaks Ranch is a country inn where you can stay in a log house and enjoy the atmosphere of a working cattle ranch. The film industry has found it an ideal setting for movies and television shows such as *The Waterboy, Sheena, Queen of the Jungle*, and many independent productions. Big Oaks Ranch, with its location in Chuluota, offers both the Center for Nutritional Studies and Agriculture Studies Center for his patients and guests.

I asked Quentin if he could give us the benefit of his wisdom on what he is famous for, diet and nutrition.

"It's simple," he said. "Eat all the fresh fruit you want every day. Limit your calories to approximately 1,500 per day, and limit your intake of sodium."

In talking to him in his office, where he still practices his health and nutrition coaching, he clearly articulated his passion for helping people get healthy through lifestyle and fitness. As he sat on his walker, talking to me in his office, sharing his inspiration and wisdom, I realized how blessed I was to have such wisdom from this medical practitioner who never allowed his physical situation to limit his contributions to our generation.

Cynthia Prince, 93

Cynthia Prince was born in Washington, D.C., on April 27, 1923, and has lived in the Ponte Vedra, Florida, retirement community of Vicars Landing for the past 28 years. Her father was an army officer and her mother taught Latin. A military family, they moved around a lot and Cynthia spent most summers at the home of her grandmother, who was a doctor. World War II came along when Cynthia was in her teens, and the summer visits to grandma's home stopped because of gas rationing.

Cynthia Prince

Cynthia's first husband was Ted Ayers, a television producer who was responsible for one of CBS television network's longest-running news programs, *Face the Nation*, until his death at age 45. They met during World War II when he was in the Air Force and had come to Smith College where Cynthia was enrolled as a student.

"He died with no money," says Cynthia, which posed a bit of a problem. She got a job as Dean of Girls Faculty Housing at a girls' day school just outside of Washington, DC. In 1969, Cynthia married Greg Prince, an executive vice president and head of the legal department for a railroad. He died in 1994.

I asked Cynthia what her dream retirement was.

"I guess I am still living it," she said.

In 1988 she began reading to children in public schools.

"I love doing it," she said. "They didn't have a structured program for reading or storytelling, so I went to the principal and started one with other volunteers in the community. It is very satisfying to read aloud to children in the classroom."

She also volunteers to read to anyone who wants to be read to at the Vicar's Landing Health Center.

When asked what she attributes her longevity to, Cynthia told me that her grandmother lived to age 95 and her sister to age 96.

"I guess it runs in the family," she said. "I exercise twice a week. I walk every day. It keeps my mind alert.

"What is the one piece of advice you would give individuals planning for retirement?" I asked.

Cynthia said that women especially should plan for the future. "Don't sit back and wait to be saved," she admonished.

"Any other advice?" I asked.

"Find time for faith," she says. Cynthia is a regular attendee at services held at the health center at Vicars Landing. "Stay active in your community. There are so many opportunities to reach out to others every day."

"Don't be a *ME* person," she said. "Don't get preoccupied with yourself."

Cynthia said that when she was a little girl, she remembers that her parents would never allow complaints. They had jobs during the Great Depression when jobs were hard to come by. She still tries hard to live up to their values.

"What do you worry about at this point in your life?"

"Well, the dollar bill is ruining this country," she said. "I worry about the environment. I worked on getting the recycling program here at Vicars and now they do. I'm proud of that accomplishment."

What keeps Cynthia going at her age are the social connections she has made in the community in which she lives. She remains active, engaged and socially connected. She loves life and considers each day a gift. I will long remember the energy that emanated from her smiling face. She smiles with her inner spirit, and it is as authentic in her love for life as it gets.

BETTY MAE COFFMAN BROWN, 92

Betty Mae Coffman Brown grew up in Defiance, Ohio, where she was no stranger to hard work. She helped her husband run the family farm. She tended a garden, canned her own food, milked cows by hand, and worked in a local factory to earn money. After she was hurt in an accident at the plant, she and her husband decided to escape the cold Ohio winters and move south to Jacksonville, Florida.

Betty Mae Coffman Brown

Betty Mae said hard work and commitment to family life are the main components to her long life so far. She and her husband were parents to six children, one having died at a week old. As of the writing of this book, she has 16 grandchildren, 33 great-grandchildren and one great-great-grandchild.

"My calling was my family," she said.

Betty Mae told me she never wanted to get married, but she fell in love. Then her husband couldn't stop "running around" on her.

"He left me after 40 years of marriage," she said. "After that, all I could think of was how to keep the family together as long as I could."

A very spiritual woman, she turned to prayer.

"I got down on my knees and got with the Lord, cried, and He delivered me from the emotional pain I was feeling," says Betty Mae. "After that, I didn't harbor anger at him and I was at peace with it all. I just kept going, and kept on working hard."

She told me she reads her Bible every day, first thing in the morning, and prays for everybody, especially her family.

Betty Mae and her husband owned a restaurant for eight years.

"He wanted to own the restaurant, but I did all the work," she said. "One day, I just walked out and left him with it. He let it go."

Betty Mae takes lots of vitamins and keeps active. She is a member of local garden clubs and has had leadership positions over the years in Eastern Star. She stays mentally active with jigsaw puzzles, puzzle books, television game shows (she calls the rest of it TV junk), and sports programs. She loves interacting with her grandchildren and never passes up an invitation to go on vacation with her children. For exercise, she loves climbing stairs.

"What advice would you give individuals planning for retirement?" I asked her.

"Accept what comes along," she said. "Don't get bitter if it brings misery. Take care of yourself. See the doctor and do what he tells you."

Betty Mae advises women against marrying for convenience.

"You have to like yourself," she says. "If anything makes you miserable, get rid of it."

Betty Mae says she doesn't worry about anything at this point in her life. She still has a life insurance policy and keeps up the premiums on it. Simple things bring her joy. Although living independently in her own wing in the home, she enjoys living with her daughter and son-in-law, and considers it a blessing to be surrounded by family. She calls all her grandchildren, great-grandchildren and her great-great-grandchild her "kids."

"I love being around them," she said. "Little Daniel comes to the staircase when he hears me coming down the stairs. I love the sound of my granddaughter practicing gymnastics in her room. I love it all."

Betty Mae believes in one step at a time. When she had trouble walking, she got a walker. "I was not going to stay behind. I want to get around," she said. But the walker was temporary. The many times I have seen her, the walker was nowhere to be seen, and she still walks up and down the stairs unassisted daily.

"There is no use in sitting around whining over things. Take things as they come and work through them," she said. "Just get things done.

At age 92, as of the writing of this book, Betty Mae says that her values have changed. She no longer places great value on things. She gives them away to her kids. She says she has concerns about the new generation coming up. They place way too much value on things and not on the simple pleasures of life and relationships with one another. She disdains the preoccupation people in the 21st century seem to have with electronics and modern technology.

"Be careful of Facebook," she warns. "What you put out there could come back to hurt you."

BOBBIE WEST, 100

Bobbie West is 100 years old, but she says she doesn't feel any different today than she did when she was 65. Born July 11, 1916, in Binghamton, New York, she worked hard all her life until her retirement in 1980. She and her husband moved to Seattle, Washington, built a house, and lived there for 15 years. He died in 2001 and she moved to Vicars Landing, a sprawling retirement community in Ponte Vedra Beach, Florida, "to just do nothing."

To Bobbie, age is just a number. She has the mindset of a much younger person. "Just open your eyes and see the sun," she says. She attributes her longevity to genes, engagement, environment, nutrition, and attitude. She stays active and motivated to share her many talents with others every day through reading.

"What is one piece of advice you would give individuals planning for retirement?" I asked her.

"No matter how much you have, you will never have enough," she replied. "Before he died, I asked my husband to teach me how to be a widow. I meant financially. He always paid the bills and handled the investments. He would never have taught me if I hadn't asked."

Bobbie keeps herself physically strong by swimming, working out and walking. Her mental strength is sharpened by reading. She is a contributing writer to the retirement community's weekly newspaper, *Vicars Voice*. She loves writing what she calls "Mom's Memoirs" for her children in which she describes key events in her life. She also writes a letter to her husband every year.

Bobbie West

"He can't read them, I know," she said, "but it's my way of keeping him alive in my mind and heart."

Her spiritual strength is augmented by study and meditation.

"Don't be afraid to die," advises Bobbie. "You shouldn't be if you have had a good, long life. I have been blessed with good health all my life, but my eyes are failing. I am at peace with what comes next."

Bobbie talks matter-of-factly about the desperate state of world affairs.

"I can't stand what's happening in the news these days," she says.

Bobbie picks a place for her kids' birthdays every year and they go someplace alone. One of the keys to her longevity, she says, is paying attention to routine and handling details. She knows what each day brings and depends on a schedule.

"Get invited out every night during the week, and then crash on the weekends," she says with a laugh.

Among her mantras are:

"Don't give up; it can get better."

"Have a strong faith."

"Don't sweat the small stuff."

"Don't be afraid to die."

"I think I have a personal guardian angel who takes care of me," she says.

Dr. James J. Rue, 92

Laguna Woods Village, a 55-plus community in sunny southern California between Costa Mesa and Irvine, has 1,800 residents (average age, 78) and 120 clubs and social organizations. I met Dr. Rue in Laguna Woods Village, the community featured in Leslie Stahl's 2014 *60 Minutes* documentary mentioned in Chapter II of this book. I had lunch with him and six other Laguna Woods residents to learn from them what I needed to know to help others

Dr. James J. Rue

Jim was born in St. Luke's Hospital, Kansas City, Missouri. When he was two weeks old, the doctor said that Jim wouldn't live because he had double pneumonia.

"The doctor was a practicing Catholic," said Jim, recounting the story his parents shared with him. "He called in a priest to give me last rites. But everyone was praying for me and those prayers worked. I am here today over 90 years old."

He shares his story graciously and inspires others by the energy and love of life he shows.

Jim's family moved to California when he was 15. His father traveled as a baseball umpire with the American League and, after spending a few summers in California, he liked it so much he moved the family there. They have been there ever since. Jim graduated from Washington State University in 1954 with a Bachelor of Arts degree in communications. He then obtained a master's degree and a Ph.D. in communication arts from University of Southern California. After teaching at USC for four years, he began working in the field of radio and television broadcasting in California and Louisiana.

Jim began working with CBS in Los Angeles as an assistant promotion and research manager for the Columbia Pacific

Network. He was also with Paramount Pictures, KTLA-TV, and NAFI Broadcasting and Syndication, a company owned at the time by Bing Crosby and Kenyon Brown, who also owned KCOP-TV in Los Angeles.

Jim was always a consummate family man. When he received an attractive offer to go back to CBS, he turned it down because it would have meant moving his family of 10 to New York City.

"I knew that once I turned down a network position like that, they would never ask again, but it was the right thing to do," Jim said. It was at this point in his life that he decided to go into teaching, counseling and private practice. While he was still working on the business end of television, he prepared himself with more courses in psychology and marriage and family counseling, and opened up his practice.

In his usual thoughtful and deliberate manner, he visited eight major cities and talked to the bishops of the Catholic dioceses before founding Sir Thomas More Marriage and Family Clinics of Southern California, with its main office in the ghetto area of East Los Angeles, and other offices in Downey, Huntington Beach, Panorama City, and Redondo Beach. The practice employed 15 counselors. He retired as president of the organization at age 65, but stayed on as chairman of the board of directors. He closed the practice in December, 2014, after 50 years of service.

Jim was married for 63 years to his wife, Cathryn, before she passed away in 2008.

"Her nickname was 'Humpty' because that's what her grandfather called her," Jim said. The couple met when he was a senior at St. Anthony's School in Long Beach, California. When World War II came along, their courtship was interrupted when Jim served in the military. They were married Aug. 5, 1945.

He beams when he recalls the close relationship they shared.

"I was a basket case after she died," he said. "I was depressed and I only wanted to be around my children. I was no longer comfortable in the presence of our 'couple' friends."

Jim says that his dermatologist helped him snap out of his depression.

"He asked me, 'Would Katie (her other nickname) want you to feel like this? She would want you to lead your life and be happy, not walking around depressed.'"

He said he bounced back and began playing golf, traveling and spending time with friends and family.

Jim still leads an active life. He still drives and dates occasionally. He stays busy keeping up with his five daughters. As to the secret of his longevity, Jim points to the fact that his grandfather lived to be 95, his father to age 88 and his mother to 92. He also credits "happiness, laughter and lots of love."

"Love someone or something you are passionate about," he says. "Have passion for something."

"What is one piece of advice you would give individuals planning for retirement?" I asked.

"Buy life insurance," he replied. "I bought life insurance for my family of 10 early on. It was my way of protecting them in case I couldn't be there to do it."

To keep physically fit, Jim swims, plays golf, visits the gym daily, and takes the stairs instead of the elevator whenever he can.

I asked Jim how he managed to stay connected with his children, since they live all over the United States. He told me that, once each week, they all have a conference call.

"The kids dial into a conference line from wherever they are and we all keep up with each other," he said. "Distance doesn't have to mean absence."

TRUMAN HERMANSEN, 99

Of all the people I interviewed for this book, one of the most interesting was Truman Hermansen, a resident of Fleet Landing in Atlantic Beach, Florida. A story on him appeared in the *Florida Times Union* on Feb. 6, 2015, written by Amanda Williamson, showing him sitting in the navigator's seat of a B-17G Flying Fortress. Hermansen flew a B-17 bomber during World War II over Germany and still has vivid memories of his experiences and those of his war buddies.

Truman Hermansen in cockpit of
restored B17-G Flying Fortress
Photo courtesy of Fleet Landing

"For 300 miles one-way, Truman Hermansen flew his United States B-17 bomber unescorted through German air space," wrote Williamson. "He still remembers the clouds of smoke, so thick he thought maybe he could walk on them, outside his plane."

Truman was only 24 when World War II began, but he volunteered and ended up training as an aviation cadet. After earning his wings, he spent the rest of the year flying bombers, one of the war's most dangerous jobs and one from which only half the men involved survived.

When Truman moved to Fleet Landing from North Carolina, it was a retirement community exclusively for veterans, and he was among the first to live there. That was 25 years ago. He loves putting around in his golf cart, playing pool, and talking over old times with his pals.

Truman and his twin brother were born in Bronx, New York, in 1917, and grew up there. As a young man, he worked for his uncle's electrical contracting firm in New York City earning $25 per week, and he always had dreams of flying airplanes. When the war came along, it was a perfect opportunity to do just that. He left New York and his fiancée behind and was off to England and flight school. The United States had not entered the war yet, but that would change when the Japanese bombed Pearl Harbor on Dec. 7, 1941.

"I learned to fly at the same field where Lindberg took off for Paris," Truman said. "In fact, my first solo flight takeoff was at the same spot on Roosevelt Airfield."

He was soon assigned to the Army Air Corps as an air cadet. He called his sweetheart in Pelham, New York, and asked her to come out to California so they could get married. She boarded a train, crossed the country, and they were wed. He was assigned to fly the B-17 bomber. He wanted to fly the larger and faster B-25, but was happy just to have an opportunity to fly.

"I wanted to bomb Berlin and get rid of Hitler for the world," he said. "We got to bomb Berlin one time. Most of the time we flew over the Ruhr Valley and dropped our payloads."

"At first I was with the 100th bomb group in the Third Division," Truman said. "Then they moved me to the 42nd bomb group. We were flying daytime raids and wiping out all their factories. That's really what ended the war. They couldn't continue to wage war if they couldn't manufacture tanks, guns and bombs."

After Germany surrendered, Truman said he and his fellow-pilots were assigned the task of flying their planes back to America where they would be outfitted for action in the Pacific Theater against Japan.

"I flew from Greenland to Hartford, Connecticut. I couldn't wait to see my dear wife whom I hadn't seen for three years," he said. By her side was his daughter whom he had never seen, not even when she was born. His oldest daughter, Gail, now lives in New York, and her younger sister lives in Connecticut.

Truman says he can still remember as if it were yesterday, all the flak exploding around his plane. At certain altitudes, the clouds of black smoke were so thick you felt as if you could get out and walk on them. Each cloud was a bomb blast hurling razor-sharp shrapnel in all directions. A piece of shrapnel pierced the aluminum skin of his B-17 on one mission, narrowly missing him.

"I was lucky," he said.

He was married for 62 years and still lives a very purposeful life at Fleet Landing. He is an active participant at the happy hours where he "sits with eight girls." Truman reports that life is great and that he enjoys his relationships with all the residents of his community.

Truman said that when he first retired, he traveled the world and "just did stuff." When I asked him what he attributes his longevity to, he shared the following insights:

"Never think about dying. Life is so great. Fill yourself with happiness. In my mind, I will never die."

Truman also advocates staying as active as possible. He works in his workshop, sews and does alterations.

His one piece of advice to individuals planning retirement had nothing to do with financial matters, travel, planning or investing.

"Keep a smile on your face, a smile in your heart. Be good to everyone and they will be good to you," he said.

Truman maintains his physical strength with love and joy—it doesn't cost a dime. His only worry comes from wanting his family to stay close to him. Other than that, this great man of wisdom doesn't worry—he's always happy. And he leaves us with the best wisdom of our time: Do unto others as you would want them to do unto you; if they don't do it for you, it's unfortunate for them!

GILBERT SCHULER, 93

Gilbert Schuler is 93 years old as this is written, and is a wonderful example of aging with grace and style. Many know him as the "Music Man of Bonnie Blink." Bonnie Blink (Scottish for beautiful view) is a Masonic Homes continuing care retirement community located in Hunt Valley, Maryland. The title fits, because Gilbert Schuler is an accomplished musician who uses his talent to entertain his fellow residents on a weekly basis.

On the day he was interviewed, it had been more than 80 years since he had taken his first saxophone lesson—something for which his dad paid the princely sum of $35 in 1935. Gilbert saw to it his father got his money's worth, practicing at least two to three hours every school day, and eight hours a day on the weekends and in the summers. My associate, Abigail Vega, had the pleasure of seeing him play a 75-minute set with no breaks except for sips of water. The set easily included 35 songs, all from memory. She described it as an amazing display of energy and talent from this member of the Greatest Generation.

The Bonnie Blink continuing care retirement community is available to Masons and their families.

Gilbert Schuler

Over the years, Gilbert has played at more events—weddings, conventions and other celebrations—in the Baltimore, Maryland, area than he can remember. His 10-piece band was known as the Gill Monroe (his stage name) Orchestra. He once owned the Gill Monroe Music Store in Overlea, Maryland, where he gave music lessons.

He enjoys using his musical talent to make people happy, he says. He has played at the Baltimore Convention Center, the Baltimore World Trade Center, and several luxury hotel ballrooms.

All one has to do is hear a few minutes of Gilbert singing in his rich, mellow baritone voice to know why he is popular. But what blows people away is how adept he is on the tenor saxophone, alto saxophone and the clarinet.

Gilbert is in good health and good spirits for his age, although he now uses a walker and has lost hearing in one ear. When I asked him what the secret of his longevity was, he told me that he has never smoked and was never a drinker, although he did work in a lot of venues where people did.

Gilbert was born in Highlandtown, Maryland, in 1922. His parents, William and Ethel Schuler, called a midwife to the home to deliver him. He had two brothers, one of whom (Albert) played the drums for Bing Crosby's orchestra in Hollywood.

Gilbert studied the saxophone under Hank Levy, a professor at Towson University, and learned the keyboard from Eddie Long, a private piano teacher. He has been a member of the Knights Templar for 66 years and has achieved the rank equivalent to a 32nd-degree Mason. He moved into the Bonnie Blink facility in January 2014 where he performs at Happy Hour between 3 to 4 p.m. on Fridays. He typically plays the saxophone while residents enjoy cake and punch. He can remember hundreds of songs. Among his favorites are Broadway show tunes, and sing-along oldies like "Slow Boat to China," "Stardust" and "Over the Rainbow." In 1965 he played tenor saxophone for Stevie Wonder's band when he performed in Baltimore.

Bonnie Blink resident Elinor Causey is Gilbert's special friend. She met him at a Happy Hour and asked him if he knew an obscure song: "In Heaven There Is No Beer."

He did know it. Elinor told him that every pub she had ever been in played that tune and "Danny Boy." But what made Elinor cry was when Gilbert later played a love song he had written especially for her and sang it for her last Christmas.

"I found my true love at 93," he says. "She is my 'Olivia de Havilland.'"

Elinor, 87, is a retired school teacher who moved to Bonnie Blink five years ago.

"Gilbert has a regular fan club at Bonnie Blink," said Elinor. "He makes CDs for people with songs by Bing Crosby, Perry Como or whoever their favorite singers are."

While the Music Man of Bonnie Blink led an amazing life as a musician, he is no "one hit wonder." He had a successful career at Martin Marietta, a leading supplier of cement and heavy building materials. He was also a member of the 175th Infantry, Company 8 in the Maryland National Guard for many years. He taught music at the prestigious McDonough Prep School for a decade, and then worked with special needs children at a school run by the Baltimore Recreation and Parks Department.

He is a man of so many talents who is committed to share them with anyone he encounters. When you interact with him, you walk away feeling inspired because of his high energy and passion for life. He plays music just to make people happy. When asked what he places the greatest value on at this time in his life, he points to his health, being happy, smiling, laughing, staying active, and living every day to its fullest. Elinor says he "wakes up happy every day"—a life lesson that no doubt contributes significantly to longevity.

NADINE SHELBY SHRAMM, 84

Nadine Shelby Shramm is an entrepreneur whose motto is: "To be successful, you need to love what you're doing. Find what you love."

Born on a Charleston, Arkansas, farm at the height of the Great Depression, Nadine grew up at a time when hard work was just what you did. She is the sixth of 11 children. She is no stranger to both adversity and accomplishment. She is a published author, and her book, *Unfinished Business—The Mother Trucker,* describes her journey from life as an Arkansas farm girl to a business mogul in New York City. In her memoir, she tells how by the age of 12 she learned to plow behind two

1,600-pound horses with her blind father walking alongside. Her father's blindness was an incurable hereditary disease, *retinitis pigmentosis*, which also caused blindness in half of the family's 10 children. Nadine counts her gift of sight as one of her most precious possessions.

"My parents taught me that 'can't' should not be a word," says Nadine. "I never forgot that."

Nadine Shelby Shramm

Nadine is very open about her first husband, who she says abused her physically and mentally during what she calls, "12 years of hell." Raped and beaten, she says she stayed in the relationship out of fear as many women do. "But I survived," she says, "and became a much stronger woman."

Nadine started her first business, one of five she would own and nurture to success, and gained enough confidence to leave. She met her second husband, Bud Shramm, at a business meeting. She was instantly attracted to him. "I was thinking to myself how lucky some woman was to be married to him," she said, "only to find that he was in divorce proceedings." They were married three years later in 1968.

"Total bliss for 23 years, and then I lost him to a massive heart attack on Dec. 23, 1990, and my world changed drastically," she added.

Bud's father, who had come to America at age 16, started with nothing but saved up enough to buy a horse and cart and start a coal-hauling business in the Chelsea district of Manhattan. That small enterprise grew to a large trucking and warehouse firm that catered to the theatre industry located nearby, a company of which Bud (Louis C. Shramm), his grandson, eventually became president. Nadine, who now found herself solely responsible for the company and its employees, did not flinch at the task. A businesswoman in her own right, she took the wheel of Budd Enterprises and increased the size of the fleet from seven vehicles to 82. She then founded Budd Leasing, Ltd., to meet the growing needs of the movie and television industries in the New York metropolitan area.

I asked Nadine, to what did she attribute her longevity?

"I love to work and I keep a positive attitude," she said. "Things happen. And when they do, you just deal with it. Don't wallow in sorrow. I am very strong. I work like a man."

Nadine keeps physically active. She walks 80 blocks at a stretch in the streets of New York City. She says weather doesn't matter; you just do it. As we walked to dinner, she stepped light as an angel in her Ralph Lauren dress, and her high heels clicking on the cracked sidewalks of New York City, I observed that Nadine has a great pair of legs for a woman her age. If you didn't know her age, you would think she was a 20-something. We laughed about that. I asked how she keeps her legs so shapely.

"I never take cabs," she said. "I walk wherever I need to go."

She reads a lot, too, which keeps her mentally active. She doesn't worry or get upset over anything. As for her spiritual life, she says she does have spiritual strength, but is not a spiritual person. She believes in doing good and always doing right, so she doesn't feel the need to sit in church. She just lives her spiritual life in her daily personal and business activities.

Nadine says she has never used being a woman as an excuse to be treated any differently in the corporate world than men. She didn't go to college. Her father needed the children to work on the farm. She remembers her father as an intelligent man, although blind. He listened to recordings of books and newspapers constantly.

"He taught me geometry using matchsticks," she said.

The secret of Nadine's long and prosperous life so far is her love of life. She does not wear her worries on her shoulder, but just lets go of them. Her greatest advice is to work through your emotions, and don't let them eat at you. She surrounds herself with good friends. She has a large, close family—11 brothers and sisters—and does not allow herself to be around needy people because "they wear you down". This, she says, is her secret—good friends, family, loving the life you have and staying active mentally and physically.

DULCE ANAYA, 84

"Dulce Anaya's influence on the
Jacksonville ballet scene is still strong"
By Kristie Andres
(Reprinted with permission from *The Florida Time Union*)

As she dismounts her teaching stool and approaches the ballet bar, Dulce Anaya stands a mere 5 feet tall.

But 50 years ago, on stage, you would believe she possessed the height of a supermodel. Her chin is lifted, eyes gazing up, and the fluorescent lights of the studio illuminate her porcelain skin as she stretches her ballerina neck long like a swan.

Dulce, whose prima ballerina days are long gone, still retains all of her ballerina glamour throughout her 39 years of directing the Jacksonville Ballet Theatre. Decorating her neck is an elaborate green-stoned necklace set in silver which, if placed on her head, would better resemble a crown of jewels. Matching silver bracelets cover her arms almost wrist to elbow. Nothing in her appearance would lead you to believe she was anything aside from a stereotypical ballerina beauty, until your eyes travel down to what she holds in her hand—a 49-cent McDonald's hamburger.

Dulce Anaya
Photo by John Pemberton/
the Florida Times Union

At age 7, Dulce, of Havana, Cuba, was already standing high on her toes like a real ballerina, or so she thought. Her mother, Dulce Ventayol, a Cuban schoolteacher with a great appreciation for theatre, took her to study under George Milenoff and Alicia and Alberto Alonso at Sociedad Pro-Arte Musical. Her mother told them Dulce could stand on pointe, but she had no pointe shoes. Dulce would perform little bourrées across the studio floor over the tops of her toes' knuckles, a painful sight that made the Alonsos cringe. Dulce soon learned how to correctly stand on her toes when she earned her first pair of pointe shoes at 7 years old.

"I could do three pirouettes on pointe, but I was all turned in," Dulce said.

Alicia Alonso made Dulce take off her pointe shoes and start again in flat ballet shoes. Alicia pushed Dulce and helped her achieve her later perfect ballerina turnout.

Dulce never had a perfect ballerina physique. She didn't have the height, the extensions, the natural turnout or the feet for ballet. She had to work harder than the other naturally talented girls, she said. Her height worked against her, especially when dancing for choreographers such as George Balanchine. She remembers thinking, "I look like a midget with all these big people," she said. "They are going to chew me alive."

In 1947, Dulce started her professional career as a ballet dancer at age 15, dancing in New York City for American Ballet Theatre, which was called Ballet Theatre at the time. She said she remembers getting over her homesickness by sending photos and letters 21 pages long to her father, Hugo Wohner, an Austrian pianist, back home in Cuba. Despite the distance from her family, Dulce embraced her independence and freedom. Because at ABT she was surrounded by professionals and dancers much older than she,

Dulce began to act and dress older than her age, which made her appear and feel as old as the other ballerinas.

When she studied under Balanchine at ABT, she remembers Balanchine telling her father, "She [Dulce] is very good, but too short and her hips are too big for her body."

Dulce was only 94 pounds at the time. Still, she did not let this criticism hold her back. She later landed a leading role in Balanchine's ballet over a veteran soloist.

Dulce, then known as Dulce Wohner, not only had to work on making herself physically appear more ballerina-like, she also had to change her last name. As her career took off, she was asked to pick a more ballerina-sounding name that was more versatile to different languages. Dulce said she opened the phone book and decided on the name Anaya because it was the same pronunciation in several languages and she was tired of being last on the list because her name was stuck at the end of the alphabet.

When ABT closed in 1948, Dulce returned to Havana and toured Latin America with Ballet De Cuba, dancing again for Alicia and Alberto Alonso. During this extensive tour, she was promoted to ballerina, which meant she gained leading ballerina status roles. When ABT reopened in 1951, she toured the United States with the company. Fred Favorite, a former ABT School dancer, said he remembered the time Lucia Chase was the director at ABT.

"Lucia wanted everyone to appear more American, so she colored Dulce's dark hair blonde," he said.

Dulce then did a long South American tour with Ballet De Cuba, and her first husband, Alberto De La Vega, accompanied her. During the tour, the company found themselves stuck in Chile because they had no money to return home to Cuba. The company left one person in Chile to stay with the costumes. They could not afford to transport them, and the rest of the 45 company dancers moved on to Buenos Aires where they were stranded for three months with no work and insufficient funds. Dulce's husband Alberto decided to step in and help the company find work. He went to Gen. Juan Perón and explained their situation. Perón, who admired Dulce, said it was no problem. He called the Teatro Colón, one of the largest theatres in the world, and had the opera cancelled so the Cuban ballerina could perform with the company. Dulce said their first performance was *Coppelia* in leotards and tights (the costumes were still stranded in Chile). The company stayed in Buenos Aires for two weeks. They finally gained the funds they needed to head home to Cuba.

Dulce gained her prima ballerina status after dancing the title role of *Undine* in 1959 for the Bavarian State Opera Ballet in Munich, Germany.

"That role really made me," Dulce said.

In a *Musical Times* review of the ballet, she was given significant credit for the success of the ballet's performance in Munich and was described as "perfect in the role."

According to the article, "She is an artist with a remarkable suppleness and a certain 'unworldly' quality, coupled with an excellent technique."

Dulce remained with the Bavarian State Opera Ballet for four more years, until she was invited to the Hamburg State Opera Ballet as Prima Ballerina. She danced leading roles in ballets such as *Swan Lake, Giselle, The Sleeping Beauty, Coppelia* and *Les Sylphides*.

Dulce was able to transform herself into a credited prima ballerina, but to this day, she has an issue with being on time. Fred Favorite said he recalls Dulce in the 1950s showing up at ABT at 1:30 p.m. for a 1-o'clock rehearsal. Dulce returned to the U.S. to dance in Miami, Florida, with the Ballet Concerto and then later decided to settle in

Jacksonville in 1970, when she founded JBT. Krista Boyer, a student of the Jacksonville Ballet Theatre for nearly 10 years, said Dulce is always on Cuban time. Boyer said she was always amazed how Dulce could instantly remember every variation to every classical ballet when you played the music, but she had a hard time remembering students' names.

"I was always 'my friend over there,'" she said.

Fred Favorite, who teaches with Dulce at JBT, also admires Dulce's teaching. He said he has always enjoyed working with her because they teach the same Russian style of ballet.

"Dulce has a wonderful philosophy in teaching and she is great with the young kids," he said. "She has a feeling for the capabilities of each person and helps each one individually."

Ronda Stampalia, a guest artist for JBT in its earlier years, said she can still see Dulce in the studio eating her McDonald's hamburger as she demonstrated a ballet bar combination. Stampalia, who now has ballet students of her own, said she thinks of Dulce often when teaching the classical ballet variations to her students. Stampalia said two main things she learned from Dulce that she passes on to her own students are purity of line and true artistry.

"The chance to be coached by a prima ballerina is once in a lifetime."

"She lived it, she did it and she passes it on," Stampalia said.

Author's Note: *Even though Dulce Anaya stepped away from actively dancing at age 45, she is still working. While she is rich in her artistic talents and gift of dance, she says she does not yet have enough money to retire comfortably, so she supplements her fixed income with revenues from her teaching. Her passion for dance continues. She continues to work out* *daily with the kids she teaches. Her advice to those planning for retirement is to "keep moving, have patience with one another, keep music in your life, seek to understand the problems of others, and be a lending hand or just an ear."*

To maintain her physical strength, Dulce has simply taken the words, "I can't" out of her vocabulary. "If you set your mind to something, work at it, and don't give up, you'll stay strong," she said. She is a sterling example of the power of a strong "can-do" mindset. She experienced broken marriages that left her financially devastated, but her persevering spirit enabled her to regain her financial identify using her gift of dance. At this stage in her life, her only worry is getting sick and not being able to move. After all, her movement as a professional ballerina is not only her passion, but the lifeline to her security.

IRIS APFEL, 95

Born Iris Barrel in Queens, New York, on Aug. 29, 1921, Iris Apfel is one of those people whom you cannot help but notice, not just for her accomplishments in the world of fashion, but for her indomitable spirit and joy of living. Famous for her wildly mismatched bulky jewelry, she was described by Ann Hornaday in *The Washington Post* as "a woman of singular vision," and a "one-woman cabinet of wonders."

At age 95, she shows no signs of retreating from her position as the queen of chic and eccentricity that is her trademark. Perhaps the best glimpse into her glamorous and dynamic life is the documentary *Iris*, filmed by the late Albert Maysles, which captures her frivolous side as fashion maven, but her delight in giving back as she teaches students from the University of Texas. The film, which premiered at the New York Film Festival in October 2014, also shows her shopping for the 100th birthday of her husband, Carl. Iris lost Carl a few months prior to his 101st birthday after a 68-year marriage. The documentary puts Iris's hilarious wit on display. Among the one-liners Iris has been overheard saying include:

"You don't own anything here—you just rent."

"A woman is as old as she looks, but a man is never old until he stops looking."

Iris Apfel

"If there were rules, I'd be breaking all of them."

"The best thing is getting dressed for the party, not going to the party."

"Everything I have two of hurts."

"If you hang around long enough, everything comes back."

"Don't give in to what hurts. Push yourself and keep going; you'll forget about it."

"Step out of the box. If you keep doing the same damn thing, you might as well step into a box."

"Keep walking around; it saves funeral expenses."

To say Iris dresses colorfully is like saying the Pacific Ocean is wet. She is a tapestry of color—a one-woman fashion parade. In the 1940s, she defied fashion norms by wearing jeans. Today, she dresses in designer trousers one day and flowing gowns the next, always accessorized by necklaces that are anything but inconspicuous and demure. Her oversized and mismatched beads and baubles give her the glamorous look of intrigue that is her trademark. Designated as a geriatric starlet, she is a pioneer in setting trends, being the first woman to wear jeans in the 40s. She reports that, when she wants something, she's like a dog looking for a bone. She's clearly a rare breed of fashion.

Iris studied art history at New York University and attended art school at University of Wisconsin. She is supersmart, but does not consider herself an intellectual. She got her start in the fashion industry working for *Women's Wear Daily* and was an assistant to fashion illustrator Robert Goodman. She married Carl Apfel in 1948. In 1950, the couple started a textile company, Old World Weavers, a firm which they operated until 1992. One of her loves is restorative decorating. She specialized in making reproductions of 17th- and 18th-century fabrics, and has worked on several restoration projects, including work at the White House for nine presidents: Truman, Eisenhower, Kennedy, Johnson, Nixon, Ford, Carter, Reagan and Clinton. She exudes confidence and an excitement about living that is contagious. Her madcap fashion ideas are a product from having traveled all over the world, collecting fashion articles that attracted her eye, and wearing them to high-society parties.

"When you don't dress like everyone else,
you don't have to think like everyone else"
— *Iris Apfel*

When asked about plastic surgery, she said, "Oh no! It may come out worse; everyone knows how old you are."

Iris believes one needs to keep a keen sense of history and curiosity.

"Everything is interrelated—politics, fashion," she says. "There is a reason for everything. Get yourself psyched about life."

"The fashion industry has done itself in by neglecting the 60- to 80-year-old market," she told *The Washington Post*. "You're supposed to fade away. They (older women) have the time and the economic resources. They want to go shopping."

"Fashion has this youth mania," Iris says. "But 70-year-old ladies don't have 18-year-old bodies and 18-year-olds don't have a 70-year-old's dollars."

While on a recent business trip in NYC, I met up with my niece, Debbie Farah. If you tune into the Home Shopping Network, you can often find both Iris and Debbie on screen, marketing their treasures which have been inspired by international artisans. Debbie was working on a fashion design project with Iris when I popped in. I was very much inspired by her clarity of direction. This was very apparent in her conversations with my niece. This woman is not planning on slowing down or stopping.

In my interview with her, I asked her, "What keeps you up at night?"

"Not much," she replied. "Perhaps matters relating to health. As you get older, you just adjust." Iris said, you "don't give in to what hurts. You just push yourself and keep going, and you'll forget about it." She runs her enterprise with a zest for life, working on projects (most recently one with Macy's department stores). Staying productive by keeping busy gives her the spirit of a 40-something, pursuing a newly discovered passion that she loves to do. So, it would be fitting to ask her a basic question: What advice would you give people planning for retirement? Without a pause she strikes back with, "they're idiots to think about retirement; retirement is a fate worse than death. You must have something to occupy your mind."

She recalled always hearing her mother's friend saying, "When I wake up every morning, everything I have two of, one of them hurts! If you have nothing to concentrate on, you focus on what hurts and no one should do that. When you have something you're interested in, you immerse yourself in it and you feel much better."

This is what drives Iris—it's her purposeful living and accepting the opportunities presented before her since her husband passed away. She's too busy living purposefully to think about what hurts. "Just love life, work hard, good fortune, and no junk food."

HARRY FRISCH, 93

In 1938, when Harry Frisch was a teenager, he and his brother, Alfred, were running from Nazi Stormtroopers when they invaded his native Austria. The pair escaped and eventually made their way to America. They were the lucky ones. Many of his relatives were caught by the Nazis and died in concentration camps. He and his brother escaped to Czechoslovakia. Their mother and father were out of the country when Hitler invaded and would never go back. The brothers later went to what is now Israel and served in the Israeli army.

After Israel achieved nationhood in 1948, Harry married his wife, Lilo, and, with their two young sons in tow, they came to the United States to start a new life. He started out as automobile mechanic, a trade he learned in Israel. Then in 1953 he joined his mother, stepfather and brother in operating Beaver Street Fisheries, located at 1741 Beaver Street in Jacksonville, Florida, a facility that today covers more than two city blocks, employs around 400 people, and has grown to become one of the country's leading distributors of frozen seafood products. Harry's oldest son and his grandsons now help run the business. His brother died in 2004.

*Harry Frisch with
author Jeannette Bajalia*

"Our family was wealthy," Harry told me. "I got away with one pair of pants, my father's watch, and a watch I got for my Bar Mitzvah."

"When we were living in Israel, we went to see a Betty Grable movie, *Moon over Miami*, and it just looked like America was such a land of opportunity," Harry said. "So I came to Jacksonville, Florida, and opened up an auto repair shop."

Harry said that, in 1955, he had to make a decision. His stepfather died and his mother was faced with closing the fish market. He said he decided to sell his auto repair business and take his savings and go in with his brother and keep the fish market going. He still works Monday through Friday.

"I plan to retire on my 100th birthday on July 5, 2023," he quipped.

When I asked Harry to what he attributed his longevity, he said, "God in heaven—do everything right. Don't lie, cheat or steal. Your biggest asset is your family and your good health. Always have a goal."

"Don't just watch things happen," he said. Then, pointing to his head, he continued, "Think and *make* things happen."

Harry had little in the way of formal education. He left school before the 11th grade and started working when he was 16.

"My education came from my wife," he said. "She told me to use my head."

Harry is outspoken about his love for the city of Jacksonville, the place he has called home for more than 60 years. He says it is the "finest place to live" and is constant in his efforts to keep the city vibrant and flourishing by giving back. One of the most recent examples of his philanthropy came with the delivery of two water taxis that Frisch was instrumental in purchasing for the city, which sits astride the St. Johns River, to keep its water transportation system running.

A generous grant from the Beaver Street Foundation in August 2015 helped establish the Frisch Institute for Senior Care, an organization that fosters interest in younger people in caring for older adults. Harry sites healthcare for seniors as one of the areas of growing concern in America. He pointed out that Florida has one of the highest populations of 60-plus residents in America.

Harry says it brings him great satisfaction when he can help others become successful and achieve their goals. He recently became involved with friends who had lost their home. He loves helping people at random when he sees them having problems.

I asked Harry what he does to keep physically fit at his age.

"I work out twice a week," he said. "And I climb two flights of stairs twice a day."

"What do you place the greatest value on at this point of your life?" I asked him.

"These are supposed to be your golden years," he replied. "I say make them golden! Ask yourself, what can I do? Be creative. If you don't use it, you will lose it. If you have nothing to do, you won't live long."

"What does what you have to do relate to age," he continued. "I seldom think, 'I'm too old for that.'"

Harry's company culture reflects that attitude. He says he would never terminate someone because of their age. The average term of employment at Beaver Street Fisheries is 40 years, a statistic he takes pride in.

"We believe in rewarding experience," he said. "I encourage people to work beyond their retirement age. After all, age is only a number."

Harry's son is president of the company and his grandson is vice president.

RUTH CONLEY, 95

Ruth Conley

There must be something about music and the love of it that keeps you young at heart. Jacksonville, Florida, resident Ruth Conley is a lifelong supporter of music arts and a major contributor to the Jacksonville Symphony. She is an accomplished pianist and, at age 95, loves playing and singing for her neighbors at Vicars Landing, a retirement community located at Ponte Vedra Beach, Florida.

When her mother was 95, Ruth brought her mother to Vicar's Landing. Now, she is following in her mother's footsteps. One of her biggest adjustments recently was giving up her car. Two weeks prior to our interview, she had just given up driving her 7-year-old Cadillac. She is still adjusting to the change but says, "it will be fine." Even though she doesn't sport her wheels, she is quite active in her lifestyle at Vicar's Landing, and continues to give back her talents and treasures to advance the world of music.

Music has always been intertwined with Ruth's life. She worked on the staff of the Seattle Symphony, and once lived across from Lincoln Center in New York City. During World War II she performed for troops as a member of the WACS (Women's Army Corps). She says she is still living her dream retirement, despite missing that car.

To what does she attribute her longevity? Genetics, she says. Her mother lived to be 100 and her father to age 105, and both in full possession of their mental faculties. Ruth reads a lot. "I was blessed with good eyes," she says. Ruth has been the proud owner of two custom-built Steinway grand pianos. One belonged to her mother. She donated that one to Vicar's Landing after her mother died. She enjoys putting on mini-concerts featuring what she calls her protégées.

"What is one piece of advice you would give individuals planning for retirement?" I asked.

"Set goals. Do your best to strengthen our society," she replied. "And plan ahead financially."

Ruth maintains her physical strength by swimming. She is a regular visitor to the pool. Her spiritual strength comes from her regular attendance at Mass and a Presbyterian Sunday School. She has been in the same Bible class for 23 years. She says that having faith eliminates the fear of dying.

"I don't worry about anything, except that my children and grandchildren continue to love the Lord," says Ruth. "The world is not what it needs to be for kids."

Ruth is grateful to her husband for the financial foundation he created for her. Because of that, she doesn't have to worry about money. She is, however, concerned about the world we are leaving for the next generation. She worries about declining moral standards and what the kids watch on TV.

Ruth has often been the recipient of honors and awards for her generosity in support of music. In 2010 she received the University of North Florida Music Department's Presidential Medallion award for her contribution to the school's music program. She is a founding member and former president of the UNF Classical Music Board, and helped establish a classical music distinguished professorship in 1998. More recently, Ruth has also supported the opera and choral program by providing scholarships for choral students and the opera program's month-long performance of Mozart's *Magic Flute* in the Czech Republic.

Ruth says that when she experiences a setback, she just keeps going. She gives the example of when she fell at age 80.

"Strive to stay independent," she said. "That's why I stay so active, especially with my music."

Ruth goes to the Vicar's Healthcare Center, where her sister-in-law is, on a daily basis and volunteers. She exemplifies the commitment of her generation to faith and family. She adds yet another priority to her life—one to which she attributes her longevity —the gift of music. The symphony.

Bob and Lee Seymour, 93 and 91

At age 93, Bob Seymour plays tennis three or four times a week and is often given the distinction as the "oldest player" in tournaments. He began playing when he was 12 years old and, at age 90, was ranked No. 1 in the Men's United States Tennis Association 90s singles division. He is currently ranked No. 4 among the 20 people in the country who play competitive tennis in his age group. "Some younger fellows came along," he says. He was born March 29, 1923. Bob's wife, Lee, is 91 and supports him in his competition.

Bob Seymour, Tennis Champion

Bob downplays the impact he has had on professional tennis. But as he moved up the ranks while advancing in age, additional age brackets had to be created. Even though he says he has slowed down playing professional tennis, by the middle of 2016, he had already played in four tournaments. From age 65 to age 90, he averaged 10 tournaments per year.

Before Bob retired in 1986, he was an accountant and comptroller of a manufacturing company in Sausalito, California. He says he always dreamed he would travel and play tennis. Now he is living his dream. He was raised in northern California and then retired in the southern part of the state where the climate was sunnier and warmer.

Lee says she loves doing the driving on the couple's tennis trips and taking care of Bob. Bob attributes his longevity to good genes and the fact that Lee makes sure they eat the right foods and get plenty of rest. Obviously, exercise is not a problem for either of them. Lee has a sister who is 90 years old and in good health. The couple married relatively late in life. He was 35 and she was 33.

Bob is a veteran of World War II and served in the United States Marine Corps from 1942 to 1946. He graduated from the University of California at Berkeley with a degree in accounting. He met Lee in 1957 while she was teaching at a girls' school in San Francisco. They have two daughters who are both in their fifties.

"I was always a stay-at-home mom when I wasn't traveling with Bob," says Lee. She now goes to exercise class five days a week sponsored by Laguna Woods Village, the retirement community in which they live. In addition to playing tennis, Bob goes to the gym twice per week and does a little hiking on the side.

"What advice would you give individuals planning for retirement?" I asked.

"Never slow down. Keep moving and stay active," Bob said. "Get some hobbies," Lee chimed in. "His is tennis, and mine is keeping up with him. Keep moving and you stay healthy."

Bob and Lee love to play cards. Two games of gin rummy every night after dinner. Lee does crossword puzzles every morning. Bob keeps track of the financial affairs of the family and looks after the investments.

"That's mental exercise," he says.

For the last six years, they have been going on trips as a family; just Bob and Lee and their two daughters. The most recent trip was to Maui for a Hawaiian cruise. Their son died unexpectedly six years ago.

"That was hard to take," said Lee, "but we got through it by just hanging in there."

"We aren't party people," Bob said. "We lead an active, simple life. Lee and I have an arrangement to go out to dinner two or three times a week. Lee cooks for us the other days of the week."

Bob says he has few aches and pains.

"Maybe a little arthritis, but I just overlook that and keep going," he says.

Bob says he doesn't worry about much at this phase in his life. He told me he fell just before a national tournament and hurt his back. He said he wasn't 100 percent, but his persistence got him back to 100 percent. Like many others in his generation, Bob seems to have a spirit of driving through challenges rather than focusing on the problem. Soon after his fall, he was back on the courts. He says his only worry was Lee's health and the physical challenges she is dealing with.

"I just had my driver's license renewed," he said, "and it is good to age 95!" He said he is determined to drive as long as he can.

I asked what his greatest joy was. He said it is primarily just getting out and running around the tennis court, and seeing his kids. He has plans for a family Christmas vacation in Maui—again just the four of them, Bob and Lee and their two daughters.. As far as the greatest value in his life, Bob says it is living in Laguna Woods and staying healthy. But then he attributes the ease of staying healthy to living in Laguna Woods.

Journal (now *Duke Law Journal*). His father was a patent attorney who settled in Florida after his military career. In 2004, Jerry received the prestigious Duke Alumni Award and currently occupies a seat on the Board of Visitors of Duke Law School.

Jerry was appointed by President Richard M. Nixon, and confirmed by the U.S. Senate, to the United States District Court for the Middle District of Florida in 1970. In 1975, President Gerald Ford nominated him to serve on the United States Court of Appeals in 1975, a post to which he was subsequently confirmed by the Senate. In 1972, Jerry was elected to the American Law Institute. He became a life member in 1997.

His honors are many. In 1996 he was awarded the Fordham-Stein Prize, a recognition that honors individuals whose work exemplifies outstanding standards of professional conduct, promotes the advancement of justice, and brings credit to the legal profession by emphasizing in the public mind the contributions of lawyers to society and to our democratic system of government.

Jerry is a rare breed in the judicial system and I felt honored to have the privilege of capturing his wisdom and passion for justice for all. He has received a host of awards and recognition by Jacksonville University, Duke University and Stetson University for distinguished public service and exemplary contributions to the various schools of law. Additionally, he received the Brotherhood Award in 1982 by the National Conference of Christians and Jews. In 1981, he was awarded the Silver Beaver Award by Boy Scouts of America. In addition to his professional accolades, the Episcopal Church awarded him the St. George Award for outstanding service to the Episcopal Church and to the Scouting movement.

JUDGE GERALD BARD (JERRY) TJOFLAT, 86

Meet Judge Gerald Bard (Jerry) Tjoflat, who a
the longest-serving federal appeals court judge st
service at the time of this writing. He is eligible
status, but has chosen to remain on the job.

Judge Gerald Bard Tjoflat

Born on Dec. 6, 1929, in Pittsburgh, Penn
Jerry was in the middle of his first year of law schoo
versity of Cincinnati when he received a letter on
mas Eve, 1952, instructing him to report for active
duty by January 15, 1953. The Korean War was rag
went through infantry training and was sent to speci
school. He served from 1953 to 1955 as a special a
the Counterintelligence Corps in the United States
Upon his discharge, he resumed his law school edu
He earned his LL.B. from Duke University Law Sc
1957, and then moved to Jacksonville, Florida, wh
established a private practice, which he maintaine
1968 when he was appointed to the Fourth Judicial (
of Florida. He served as associate editor of the *Du*

Modest about his contributions, he simply does what it takes to make a difference in society, another attribute of this great generation. When I asked him to what he attributed his longevity, Jerry said he tries not to overeat, and plays golf for exercise.

"I had a hip replacement a couple of years ago," he said. "That went well. I can't walk as much as I once did, but I stay active playing golf."

As this is written in late 2016, Jerry is in his 41st year of service on the courts. He explained about "senior status."

"You have three options if you are over 65 years old with at least 15 years of active service," said Jerry. "You resign your commission for full pay for life, take 'senior status,' which creates a vacancy, or you can keep working and maintain active status. I chose to keep working."

Jerry didn't take the easy way out like many do. He could be retired with a full pension based on his current salary. Typical of many of his generation, having a purposeful career keeps him going. His contribution to family and friends keeps him mentally, physically and emotionally strong.

Jerry has served in active status longer than any judge in US history, going back to 1891 when the U.S. Court of Appeals was created.

Jerry's first wife died in 1997. They had two children—a son, born in 1958, and a daughter in 1960. Their daughter was Director of Development for Mayo Clinic until she left to go into the seminary. She is now an Episcopal priest. He remarried in 1998. His current wife, Marcia, is a retired attorney and has one child from a previous marriage.

Jerry loves teaching. He has mentored 185 law clerks.

"I tell young lawyers that the world needs the wisdom of great lawyers and needs their contribution to their communities," he says. "The large legal firms make older attorneys leave to make room for younger attorneys, and in the process they lose a lot of that wisdom."

He also notes that when organizations such as the FBI force early retirement at age 55, they lose a lot of knowledge and wisdom. He frequently challenges this mindset.

Jerry believes there is much charitable work to be done. He is active in the Episcopal Church where he is Senior Warden at the Cathedral and Rector of the Parish, a position of service he has enjoyed since 1960. He is one of the founders of the Episcopal High School and serves as Director of Fresh Ministries of the Episcopal Church, an interfaith organization working to eliminate poverty and crime.

Jerry enjoys spending time with "Washington Duke," his champion black cocker spaniel, who just goes by "Duke."

I asked the judge what he worries about most.

"I worry about the under-55 generation," he said. "The overall behavior of this generation seems to show a lack of respect and reverence possessed by their parents. In general, they seem to have lost touch with their moral compass."

Among his greatest joys, the octogenarian jurist says he loves solving legal problems, having dinner with friends, playing golf, teaching law classes, and working with young attorneys who have a thirst for learning.

Jerry says he has no concept of retirement.

"If you have a purposeful career and you love what you do, why should you retire?" he says, adding that he will continue doing what he is doing as long as he thinks he is still contributing. He's in the game to stay and influence— isn't that what life should be at all life stages?

JOAN AND STEVE MILES, 97 AND 94

Joan and Steve Miles with books they coauthored

Joan and Steve Miles met in their teens and have been in love ever since. They were married in 1945 and live in Flemming Island near Jacksonville, Florida. Both are creative. He worked from 1951 to 1988 as a graphic artist at Honeywell International and oversaw its arts department. She wrote a newspaper column for the *Burlington Times-Union* in Burlington, Massachusetts. At one point, they collaborated on a column together, *she* writing the copy and *he* laying out the comic strip that went with it. They have coauthored two books. One is a story about their parents' generation, entitled *Feeding Dreams*, and the other is about a 58-year-old minister, John Muilenberg, who was pastor of a church they were attending and who lived to be 101. The book, *Charisma*, is his story. They approached their authoring projects as a team and worked together; she did the writing and he did the illustrations and the graphics. They also wrote a children's book and were gracious to share the results of their book project with me—something I will cherish because they so kindly let me into their hearts and minds.

The Mileses attribute their longevity to a happy marriage (70 years and counting). They also believe firmly in
good diet and exercise. They both work out three times a
week at the YMCA.

The couple has done a lot of traveling and are still living their dream retirement—living independently, driving,
and taking care of their home, which I found to be immac-
ulate and organized much like they present themselves.

"Other than a few problems with arthritis, we are in
pretty good shape," Steve said.

They stay mentally active, reading books, doing crossword puzzles together. They both enjoy working on their
computers and have lots of friends on Facebook. Steve
loves art and does most of his artwork on the computer.
They have two daughters in Florida and five grandchildren,
plus extended family in Barbados.

"Oh yes, we drink a glass of white wine every day," said
Joan.

"What is one piece of advice you would give individuals planning for retirement?" I asked.

"Take good care of yourself," they both agreed. "Don't
say, 'If I knew I'd live that long I would've taken better care
of myself.' Keep active in body and mind."

Joan and Steve were very frank about the future.

"We don't really worry about anything at this point
in our lives," Steve said. "Our days may be dwindling, but
why worry about things you can't control? We keep opti-
mistic. Things will be better in the future."

They enjoy reading two daily newspapers—*The Boston Globe* and *The New York Times*, both online. They even
catch an occasional baseball game. They are regulars at the
Choices class at their Presbyterian church. Choices is a
book club where they join with others in discussions on
the books they are reading. They say it helps them keep

mentally and spiritually active as the books are solely on spiritual topics such as prayer and church.

Financially, they are well set. They sold their home and put the proceeds into an annuity for monthly income. They each have pensions and Social Security. They planned well and want to leave something worthwhile to posterity when they are gone, like a scholarship fund.

They beam when they show you pictures and tell you about their family.

"Love makes the world go around," Steve said.

"At least it does for us," Joan added.

A lesson learned from the Mileses: They greet each day with a spirit of optimism, regardless of how they might be feeling, or what they are experiencing. They keep on thinking things will get better, and this gets them through.

JOE AND MARY MANCINO, 91 AND 90

Joe was born Sept. 16, 1925, and Mary, Nov. 19, 1926. They both came from the same neighborhood in the Germantown section of Philadelphia known as Cowtown, where they were childhood sweethearts since the 1930s.

"When I was 8 years old, in 1934, my father, Domenick, an Italian immigrant, opened a grocery store on a vacant lot in our neighborhood, and I helped in the store," said Mary. "Joe's family lived down the street and our family lived above the store. Joe came in and saw me and said, 'I'm going to marry you.' He was 9 and I was all of 8 years old!"

Their first actual date was when Joe was home on leave from the Navy in December 1945. Prior to that, when they were teenagers, Joe would walk with Mary when she went to the bank, or did her other chores. When Mary walked the dog, Joe would jump up and walk with her. He said he took every opportunity to be with her. They wrote to each other when he was away in the Navy. They were married in June 1947, soon after Joe left the Navy.

Joe's grandmother, also named Mary, was an excellent Italian cook. When Mary (Joe's wife) was a newlywed, Joe's grandmother showed her how to cook some of her favorite dishes. She used no measuring cups or spoons. The way she measured the amount of seasoning that went into a dish was by placing the ingredient (salt, garlic, basil, oregano, etc.) in the palm of her hand. Once poured into the hand she compared the amount to the size of a dime, a quarter or half dollar.

The author, Jeannette Bajalia, left, poses with Mary and Joe Mancino

During World War II, Joe was in the U.S. Navy and saw action in the Pacific Theater. He helped liberate the Philippines and was stationed in Australia, Pearl Harbor and Midway. He served aboard the USS Coucal, a sub tender, and the USS Griffin. He also took part in "Operation Crossroads," testing nuclear weapons off the Bikini Atoll.

Following his stint in the military, Joe returned to Germantown, where he worked in his father-in-law's corner grocery store as a meat cutter. He later joined the Penn

Fruit Supermarket chain as a union meat cutter, and was later promoted to manager of the store's meat department.

Mary worked part-time as a credit authorizations representative for Sears, Roebuck for 20 years while raising four children. Following Joe's retirement at age 65, the couple moved to Ponte Vedra Beach, Florida, in 1992.

"What was your dream retirement?" I asked.

"Just to relax and do nothing," Joe said. "Just be a bum."

Mary added that they enjoy working around their home, gardening and painting. They spend time with family. Seven grandchildren and six great-grandchildren keep them busy.

"We have always taken vacations with the children and grandchildren," Mary said. "It is one of the highlights of our lives. We still celebrate the holidays at our home."

As to the secret of their longevity and good health, the Mancinos cited eating a healthy diet and always having plenty to do.

"You never get bored if you always have something to do," said Mary.

How do the Mancinos advise couples just entering their retirement years to maintain their physical, mental and spiritual strength?

"Take 25 percent and give 75 percent," they said. "And stay in a good routine."

Mary said that they enjoy playing cards on their computers, doing word finders, and talking with each other daily over morning coffee. They watch daily Mass on television and say their rosary each evening at 7:30.

"As long as you have family, you have each other," Joe said, adding that they place the most value on family and faith these days.

"My appreciation for my parents has grown over the years," Mary said. "My father made me stay in school

114 PLANNING A PURPOSEFUL LIFE

instead of quitting and getting a job. They were very conservative people who taught us the value of hard work and saving money."

"Yeah, the older I got, the smarter my parents became," Joe said with a laugh. He said his only regret was that he didn't get a better education.

The Mancinos can frequently be seen walking around their upscale neighborhood in Ponte Ve\dra Beach, which is what they like to do for exercise.

MARY N. HALL, 91

Mary Hall was born May 29, 1925, in New Jersey and raised in Brunswick, Georgia. She has a soft spot in her heart for people and dogs. All of her professional life has been spent as a social worker and she has had 39 family dogs over her lifetime. She currently owns a golden retriever therapy dog that accompanies her to various hospitals where she visits patients as part of her ongoing social work, and raises guide dogs for the blind. She does not allow age to get in her way of continuing to pursue her passion of serving others through her social work expertise.

Although she officially retired from her paid positon as a professor at University of West Florida in 1993, she is still working, helping families deal with loss and grief through a church-sponsored caregivers group. While at UWF, she developed the department of social work.

Mary says she doesn't think about retirement.

Mary Hall

"I'm not well off, so I don't have any travel expectations," she explains. "My husband and I were homebodies." She met her eventual husband, Lester, in 1960 at a networking event in Oklahoma where he was director of the state's mental health association. He died of a brain tumor after 48 years of marriage.

Mary attributes her longevity to genetics and a "never quit" attitude she learned from her mother. She has had several bumps in the road—a broken leg, breast cancer, an umbilical cord hernia, and a shoulder replacement. Other than that, she says, she is in good health and enjoys biking, walking and swimming for exercise.

"Never let illness define you," she admonishes.

Mary stays busy in her church. She sings in the choir and volunteers at local hospitals. To stay mentally active, Mary enjoys reading and challenging herself with theology study and crossword puzzles.

"What advice would you give those on the threshold of retirement?" I asked Mary.

"This is your life. Always have too much to do, but don't miss the scenery along the way. Accept life and go forth. Take care of your body in every way and get some rest. Observe the Sabbath—it's there for a reason," she said. "Keep a sense of humor. Be with people who share things; we are not alone in this world."

"What worries you in life?" I asked.

"That I will not be able to accomplish everything I set out to do. I also worry about children. My heart goes out to them—especially those who are in need.

"It bothers me that I could die suddenly without having the opportunity to say goodbye to my family and friends," she said. Mary recently had a birthday party and 116 people showed up to help her celebrate.

"What do you place the greatest value on at this point in your life?" I asked.

"The Holy Spirit," she responded without hesitation. "The search for deeper faith. Relationships with others, friends and children. I really appreciate hugs."

Offsetting Mary's serious side is a comedic streak. When the pastor of her church recently retired, she put on a "one-person opera skit" and did a spot-on imitation of Grand Ole Opry's Minnie Pearl singing. This is an example of her greatest joy—silliness. Yes, silliness. She likes to laugh and be silly, something that keeps her spirit young and alive.

ARNOLD AND MARILYN NEILSEN, 96 AND 94

Relatively speaking, Arnold and Marilyn Neilsen are newlyweds. They met at the Scandinavian Club in Ocala, Florida (both have family roots in Denmark), in 2002 and tied the knot six weeks after their third date. They each have four children from previous marriages.

Arnold was born May 21, 1920, and Marilyn was born April 11, 1923. Arnold was a mining engineer, and Marilyn worked part time as a pharmacy technician. They both have colorful histories and many stories to tell.

Arnold served as a veteran of World War II, having fought in the battle of Iwo Jima. He was in the military for seven years, achieving the rank of Captain in the U.S. Army. After the war, Arnold raced Porsches in Lime Rock, Connecticut, obtained his pilot's license and flew airplanes in New Jersey, and sang in a men's chorus at Madison Square Garden in New York City during a Billy Graham Crusade. His work as a mining engineer took him all around the world. He has visited such far-flung places as New Zealand, Israel, Bolivia, Indonesia and New Brunswick, Canada.

Arnold and Marilyn Neilsen

Marilyn was raised in Chicago about a mile from Lake Michigan and lived there until she retired. She started working as a pharmacy tech when her children started school in 1969 and did that for 10 years. Comparing notes, Marilyn and Arnold discovered that they have been to all 50 states—Arnold traveling with his work, and Marilyn because she has children living in Colorado, North Carolina and Toronto, Canada.

I asked them my favorite question: "To what do you attribute your longevity?"

"We both have good attitudes and we are the kind of people who never look back," said Marilyn. "Never worry about yesterday or tomorrow," she advised.

They are both socially active. They attend local dances and parties and enjoy an occasional beach weekend together. To maintain physical strength, they exercise regularly.

"We have a senior center near our home in Ponte Vedra Beach with two pools, a large exercise room and a hot tub," Arnold said. "We go there three times a week and exercise."

Arnold does laps and pull-ups in the pool and lifts weights in the gym. They also participate in activities sponsored by the center.

Keeping active is no problem for the Neilsens. Marilyn enjoys knitting afghans for newborns at the nearby Jacksonville Naval Air Station hospital and together they have logged over 5,000 hours of volunteer work. They both enjoy crossword puzzles and read a lot. They dine out and enjoy the occasional boating excursion with a daughter who is a member of a boating club. Little things bring them joy, the first of which is quite simple: Each other! He exercises his sense of romance by getting up first, making breakfast and bringing her a cup of coffee in bed so she can read the paper.

"He makes breakfast in the mornings and does the dishes," said Marilyn.

"I love clutter and she doesn't," laughed Arnold.

Marilyn followed up our interview with a few thoughts she wanted to share as she started reflecting on our conversation. She wanted to make sure I was aware of four important things about her life with Arnold at this stage:

1. Saying "I love you." Although you might already know it, she says "hearing it is special."

2. Being aware of each other. Making observations like, "You look nice in that outfit." Or, "I like that shirt, the color is right for you." Or, "You look tired today. Are you OK?" Marilyn cautions that you should never let someone become invisible. Keep the feelings alive at ANY age.

3. Saying "thank you" for small things, like getting a cup of coffee, or carrying something, or putting away groceries to show you still care.

4. Accepting each other. Don't try to change each other.

Arnold and Marilyn apply these tenets to their relationship daily. When you're around them, you feel the spirit, love and commitment they have for each other. Simple wisdom from the Greatest Generation.

"What is the one piece of advice you would give individuals planning for retirement?" I asked.

"Keep active and find hobbies and interests that keep you busy and make life meaningful," they said.

"What do you worry about at this point in your lives?"

"The last thing we want to do is be a burden on our children."

In keeping with their credo, the couple stays active, including travel. Marilyn's daughter, a retired navy commander, made arrangements for Marilyn and Arnold to tour seven aircraft carriers and a nuclear submarine in Norfolk, Virginia, when she was stationed there.

"We had to get security clearance, it was so classified," said Marilyn.

LUCILLE ELLSON, 99

Lucille Ellson was born Dec. 30, 1917, while World War I was raging in Europe and America was sending its youth to the fray. She was one of seven children born on a farm in Laurens, Iowa. Her grandparents were hard-working immigrants from Sweden and Germany. She grew up doing farm chores, but her father insisted she and her siblings get a college education. Her father later became a bank president, and Lucille's grandson, who is an attorney, still owns the farm, which has now been in the family for more than 100 years. She is the second-oldest of her brothers and sisters and has outlived all of them, a fact which she says leaves a void in her life.

Education, it seems, is a family tradition. Her mother was a country school teacher. Lucille's husband, Floyd, whom she married when she was 25 years old, lived to be 104 years old, and was a school superintendent until he retired in 1975. Lucille also taught elementary school in Vinton, Iowa, for two years after she graduated from college and then went on to learn braille and teach it to the blind and sight-disadvantaged children for the next 14 years. She retired at age 63 in 1980.

Lucille Ellson

Even at this stage in her life, Lucille's passion is staying involved with braille. She still belongs to organizations that help serve sight-disadvantaged students and communities. She recently gave a talk to the seniors about braille. She told of her experiences teaching in the braille school and the new developments available for braille students. She shared stories about how blind children do things that they don't think sighted people can see them do.

"There was the one little boy who took some braille paper from the classroom to his dorm room," she said. "When I asked him what he was doing, his response was: 'I didn't think you'd see me taking it.'"

Like many of her generation, World War II interrupted Lucille's life. She met her husband when they were both teachers.

"In those days, it was in a teacher's contract that if you got married, and you were both teachers, the woman had to quit teaching," Lucille said. "That didn't make sense, but that's how it was. We knew he would probably be drafted, so we waited until he was and then got married. That way I would still have a job while he was in the Navy. He got $99 a month during the war."

In 1937, Floyd taught in a small school in Otranto, Iowa. Then he was drafted. After his military tour, the couple married and started a family. In 1945, after the war ended, they moved to Webb, Iowa, where Floyd was a teacher and a coach, and later a school superintendent. Lucille stopped teaching to raise their four children.

"We had a deal," she said, "that when the kids went to college I would go back to work."

Lucille and her husband both shared an interest in creative writing.

"He always wanted to write a book about the family and our lives and dedicate it to the kids and grandkids," she said. "He took a course in creative writing, and wanted to call the book *The First 100 Years*, about the first 100 years of our lives. When he got a computer, he started writing stories. He had a stroke at age 92, but he was still mentally sharp."

Lucille kept encouraging him to work on the book. She bought him a tape recorder and became his assistant. On his 100th birthday, one of the grandsons, who was a graphic designer, gave him a design for the book cover. Lucille says she likes it but it's "just not right yet."

Lucille says she has a large collection of stories and letters and is still working on the project. During my first visit with her, she had the book transcript nearly completed and was sorting through pictures to add to the stories. What a gift this will be to her family! She made a promise to Floyd that she would finish the book. So she is working hard to complete the project. She is healthy, active, and still living independently, but she still worries she won't be able to finish the book "before she's called home."

Lucille credits her longevity to staying active and remaining curious about life. She has a lot of energy, and has had a lot of stimulation in her life.

"Keep moving, loving and learning," she said. "We didn't smoke or drink and this helped with our health. In Iowa, it was easy to not drink, since alcohol was prohibited."

To keep herself physically strong, she enjoys housework, shopping, working with plants, line dancing, hosting and attending tea parties, and walking in the neighborhood.

For mental exercise, she plays Mahjong. She started two groups, and hosts the women weekly at her home. She trained the participants and now has a dedicated space in her home that is always set up for what she calls her "Mahjong gang."

She feeds her spiritual side by attending church as much as she can and praying often. She also participates in senior groups. Her faith has always been an important part of her life. She hosted a Bible study in her home for five years.

"I stay busy and don't think about myself," she said. She has a handicapped son who is an attorney. She says he has been financially successful and has the resources he needs for himself and his family, because he planned and saved. He was afflicted with his rare disease 25 years ago. He still comes to her home every morning at 10:30 a.m. and stays until 3 p.m. when his wife gets off work. She says she enjoys this time with her son because it helps both of them.

LOYCE DOERING, 102

At 102 years old, Loyce Doering says she considers her eyesight as one of her greatest blessings.

"I read all the time," she told me. "I read the Bible and I go to the library to get Amish books." She added that she cares little for what's on TV, except maybe the game shows which she watches from time to time.

Loyce Doering

Loyce was married to Ernie Doering in the early 1930s. They met at a party. He died in 1994. They had two sons, three grandchildren and eight great-grandchildren, all of whom live in Jacksonville, Florida, and the surrounding areas. She never worked, but stayed at home with the children.

"I did do a lot of babysitting in Ortega (a Jacksonville neighborhood) and a lot of volunteer work at St. Vincent's, a local hospital," she said.

Loyce says she is still living her dream retirement. She was still driving her car when I talked to her and is seldom at home. But she has now given up her keys. She goes to the senior center and eats lunch out a lot. She says one of her joys is going out to lunch with the girls, her friends, and staying out a long time just catching up and enjoying each other. She loves visiting with friends and family. She doesn't get to see her children and grandchildren as much as she would like. She lost her oldest son and his wife in an auto accident, and her other son stays busy with work most of the time. Relationships are what she is all about—staying

CHAPTER V | 125

connected with family and friends. She gets a lot of opportunity to do that with her network of friends.

Loyce attributes her longevity to "putting God first in my life, Bible study, and church."

She believes in eating healthy. She eats anything she wants, but no canned foods and no soft drinks—only water.

"What advice would you give people contemplating retirement?" I asked.

"There are three things that are important," she said. "The Lord, staying busy, and proper food."

Handling setbacks in life, says Loyce, is a matter of brushing them off and keeping on.

"I do a lot of walking," she said. "Last Christmas, I fell and shattered a vertebra in my neck. I had some pain, but I just take a pill for the pain and keep going."

Obstacles don't get in her way, and this seems to be a common characteristic of the Greatest Generation.

THOMAS MCCOY, 91

When I interviewed Tom McCoy for this book, I found him to be a soft-spoken, intelligent man who makes you feel very special when you are in his company. He was born on April 19, 1925, so he was a teenager when World War II erupted in Europe. When he was 19, he volunteered to fight for his country in 1943, and distinguished himself by serving in the 14th Armored Division. He remained in the Army for another year after the war ended and played football for the Army team in Germany.

Tom McCoy poses with author
Jeannette Bajalia

Tom married his college sweetheart, Margaret Beasley, in 1950. After 64 years of marriage, she passed away in 2014 from a breathing disorder at age 85. Tom says he misses her a great deal. After graduating from Auburn University in Auburn, Alabama, Tom became an insurance agent for State Farm Insurance Company in Birmingham, Alabama, and became agency manager seven years later. He subsequently rose through the State Farm ranks to become agency director in the company's regional office and was promoted again to executive assistant in the Bloomington, Illinois, home office, a position he held until his retirement in 1995. He has two daughters who adore and dote on him: Beth, who lives in Ormond Beach, Florida, and Terri, who lives in Jacksonville, Florida. He also has three grandchildren. Attending Auburn University and working for State Farm seems to be a family tradition: Both daughters graduated from Auburn University; a grandson, Luke, is currently attending, Terri worked in the insurance company's claims department for 35 years; and Beth's husband, Blake Thomas, works for State Farm in Port Orange.

Tom is a devoted fan of Auburn University sports. In honor of his 90th birthday, the city of Auburn, Alabama, declared April 19, 2015 "Tom McCoy Day," and gave him a key to the city in tribute to his financial contributions in support of athletics, his service on the National Alumni Board, and his serving as president of two different clubs associated with the University. Tom is on the board of directors for Florida Citrus Sports.

Tom walks with a cane now, and suffers from neuropathy, a condition which causes him to have little or no feelings in his legs. He also deals with an inner ear problem that affects his balance.

"I guess I just have bad wheels," he joked.

"To what would you attribute your longevity?" I asked Tom.

"My mother lived to be 92 and my father was 83 when he died," said Tom. "They were people who believed in moderation in all things. They would have a little wine now and then but never overindulged in anything."

Tom says his neuropathy keeps him from playing golf the way he would like to, but he exercises daily, doing push-ups and riding his bicycle.

"If you could give one piece of advice to individuals planning for their retirement," what would it be?" I asked him.

"Be sure you are financially ready," he said. "I retired when I was 70. I worked a little longer to make sure I was financially prepared. Whatever you dream your retirement to be may not play out. You have to be ready for anything." He experienced this when he bought a home in Cashiers, North Carolina, in 1995 when he was six months into retirement and at a time when his wife had health challenges.

"You just need to be prepared," he said.

"It's like I have always told my daughters," he continued, "try to spend the earnings, not the principal. That way you can leave a legacy behind. I made them promise they would do that."

Tom keeps mentally active by reading. He watches TV, but doesn't get "hooked" on one program, which he considers a waste of time. He is a spiritual man, having served at one time as chairman of the board of elders in the Methodist church he attended.

"My family has always been religious," he said. "My father was very active in the church. That spiritual background allows me to deal with a lot of problems. It helps me enjoy life. I have always tried to influence my daughters along that same path."

"Sixty-four years is a long time to stay happily married," I told him. "How did you do it?"

"Keep it peaceful," he said. "Walk away from heated encounters."

His peaceful spirit allows him to do that. Another key attribute of this great generation: They don't sweat the small stuff. They rise above life challenges and keep going. Mental toughness and a soft heart is "the real McCoy."

WILHELMINA BURGESS, 98

Wilhelmina Burgess was born just before the end of the First World War on May 13, 1918. A native Floridian, she grew up in Orlando when it was little more than a rural backwater that bore slight resemblance to the metropolis it is now. She still lives there, as do her two children. She has four grandchildren, 13 great-grandchildren, and one great-great granddaughter. Her husband died in 2013.

Wilhelmina thinks that perhaps longevity runs in her family. Her mother lived to age 102. When I asked her if she was living her dream retirement, she said that she and her husband of 55 years had traveled all over the world. She walked me through her home and showed me the treasures she had collected during her travels, and recalled special memories and joyful periods.

"But you reach a point when it's time to do for others," she said. "What brings me the greatest joy at this stage in my life is meeting people and living a full life."

During my conversation with Wilhelmina, I learned that she is quite active for her age. She cooks for herself and enjoys it—lots of vegetables and, as she puts it, "a lot of hot sauce for circulation." Her favorite beverages are Ensure and coffee.

"I don't drink alcohol," she said with a wave of the hand. On most days, Wilhelmina spends 20 minutes on the treadmill and does her swimming and Yoga exercises.

"I would love to have a buddy my age to exercise with," said Wilhelmina with a twinkle in her eyes, "but no one my age is around!"

Wilhelmina, or "Mina" as her friends call her, enjoys taking care of her plants and flowers and imparting an encouraging word to others she meets. She says she does her own vacuuming, even though it takes her longer to do it than it once did.

She has strong feelings about how to keep healthy at her age. She does not believe in taking a lot of drugs unnecessarily.

"You end up taking too many drugs if you aren't careful," she advises. "If you swallow a pill for every little ache and pain, you can end up taking too much medicine, and that's not good for you. I stopped smoking at age 62 and started eating right, and have been doing so ever since.

"When people say they have back pain on one side," she says, "I tell them to just sit on the other side. Pain is in the mind. Rise above your aches and pains and just live."

Wilhelmina stays mentally active and loves to learn.

"Sometimes I have to pray to the Lord to keep my mouth shut," she confesses. "I say it like I see it, and it gets me in trouble sometimes."

Wilhelmina Burgess

She has a healthy sense of spirituality, but says she prays at home and doesn't go to church.

"I do watch church programs on TV," she says, "and say my prayers in the morning and at night."

Wilhelmina was never in a hospital until three years ago when she contracted a bladder infection.

"They kept me there for seven days," she said. "When they released me, I stayed with my daughter for three days until I convinced her I was fine and went home."

"What do you worry about at this point in your life?" I asked her. "Nothing," was her reply. She says she doesn't need a lot of money, but enjoys her flowers and clothes. What brings her joy is seeing the sun come up on the horizon. She says, "that's living."

Mina is full of life and passionate about bringing value to others, but she feels "stuck" because she doesn't drive.

"I can go to nursing homes and help people," she said. "Folks like me can volunteer to help others; we still have it in us."

That kind of spirit summarizes Mina's legacy. Do not confuse her chronological age with how old she feels. Her youthful spirit and desire to serve others less fortunate than she shows that serving others cannot be predicated on age. Wouldn't it be a beautiful thing to see this generation given opportunities to volunteer their time and talents with their less-fortunate peer group?

OLEN LEVELL, JR., 1916-2016

Olen Franklin Levell, Jr. was born on July 3, 1916, and passed away Feb. 26, 2016, shortly after I interviewed him for this book. He died, as they say, with his boots on—active to the very last, with a "never quit" spirit and a twinkle in his eye. I attended his military funeral service, a befitting ceremony for a patriot who served his God, country, his family, and his fellow-man.

Olen worked for PPG Industries as an accountant, and then in marketing, a job that required traveling extensively to promote new products. He retired in 1979 at the age of 65, and he never thought his retirement would last as long as his working life. He was a trailblazer at whatever he did. When I asked him about his dream retirement and if he was still living it, he simply replied, "No specific plans. I just want to enjoy life."

He and a group of friends bought into a community in Indian Lakes, Florida, that had a nine-hole golf course, which they built into an 18-hole course. This gave him great joy because it was a project with a group of friends. He was all about people and relationships, whether it was his family, his professional associates, or all those he influenced and shared a smile with in his volunteer activities.

When I met Olen, he was still, at age 98, volunteering to help others. He worked at Flagler Hospital Pharmacy in St. Augustine, Florida, participated weekly in "Meals on Wheels," an assistance outreach for the homebound and disabled. Every week, you could find him working at the church, pulling the weekly church bulletins together for Sunday services. He read books and magazines and loved jigsaw puzzles.

His sense of humor was adorable.

"To what do you attribute your longevity?" I asked him.

"Clean living until the age of nine or 10," he quipped. Basically, his philosophy on successful retirement was simple. "Don't sit around. Keep on moving."

Olen was a member of a church group that calls itself the "Dine with Nine." They met monthly for fellowship and conversation. Albeit with the aid of his wheeled walker the last few months of his life, he would take a stroll after each meal on one of the many walking paths in his community.

"What advice would you give individuals planning for retirement?"

"Saving is your security," he said. "Save *before* you retire. Don't spend more than you earn. And when you retire, keep active."

*Olen Levell, Jr. poses with
author Jeannette Rajalia*

Olen maintained an amazing spirit of perseverance.
When I continued asking what do you do to maintain your
mental strength, he was quick to say he just simply stays
active, whether it be his formal volunteer activities or his
informal activities at the church where he acted as a greeter.
He could be seen giving out bulletins at the weekly services,
greeting each person with a big smile and a joyful spirit.

He met each adversity with a good attitude and relentless determination. That would seem appropriate for a man
who flew 28 missions in the war. Would we expect any less
from such a patriot? When he broke his hip, a few years
before I met him, he didn't let it beat him. He manifested a
great attitude, and did all his physical therapy with the determination that he would soon be walking again without
assistance. And that's what he did.

When I asked him what he worried about at this point
in his life, he chuckled and said, "Nothing; at my age, what is
there to worry about?" he responded. Then after a reflective

pause, he concluded that he supposed his only worry was that his daughter worried about him overdoing it.

He and his daughter, Ann Junod, had a great relationship—one based on the mutual admiration and a mutual love for service of others.

Olen served his country as a B-24 Liberator bomber pilot in World War II, completing 28 missions. For years, he kept up with members of his crew. With his death died a piece of history, as he was the last surviving member.

"After each mission, our crew played bridge to calm down and settle our nerves," he told me. "That, and a little scotch."

"Dad showed great love and appreciation for my taking care of him," said his daughter "I think he just didn't want to leave me. He died 12 hours after I told him that it was OK to go to God, and my stepson told him that he would look after me." And then he transitioned to his new home.

CHAPTER VI

AGE IS ONLY A NUMBER

"Too many people, when they get old, think that they have to live by the calendar."

– John Glenn

O N OCT. 29, 1998, U.S. SENATOR JOHN GLENN became the oldest person to ever fly in space when he and his fellow astronauts left earth orbit aboard the space shuttle Discovery on a nine-day mission. He wasn't just there for decoration, either. His official duty was payload specialist. Of course, it was an honor. After all, Glenn helped pioneer space exploration when NASA was just a baby. But it was a scientific journey. He was there to investigate the effects of space travel on older people. How would his 77-year-old body react to the weightlessness of space? Would it affect his immune system? His balance? His blood flow and his sleep patterns?

He circled the earth 134 times, traveling 3.6 million miles in the process and, when it was over, was none the worse for wear. Granted, his reentry was only 3 Gs, compared to the 6 Gs he experienced on Friendship 7 in February 1962. But still, he was up to the task. How well that exemplifies that we cannot let age define us or allow the calendar to hem us in. If we do, we eliminate for ourselves

potentially valuable opportunities to enjoy a rich and fulfilling life.

MORE CENTENARIANS THAN EVER BEFORE

If you are not the sort of person who is easily spooked,
old cemeteries can be great places in which to take a pleas-
ant walk and just explore local genealogy and history. St.
Augustine, Florida, is full of old graveyards. The Hugue-
not Cemetery, which is located just across from the city's
historic City Gate, was a Protestant burial ground back in
1821 when the Florida territory became a possession of the
United States.

In addition to the colorful inscriptions on some of
the monuments and tombstones, you will find the dates of
birth and death of the dearly departed. What is interesting
is how short their lifespans were. Few lived past the age of
50. Most died in their 40s. I touched on the ever-increas-
ing lifespan of Americans in Chapters One and Two of this
book. But a phenomenon that impresses more and more
demographers is just how many people in America are centenarians these days (those living to be 100 or more). According to an article written by Sabrina Tavernise in *The
New York Times* of Jan. 21, 2016, the number of Americans
age 100 and older is up by 44 percent just since 2000!

Quoting data released by the Centers for Disease Control and Prevention published in January 2016, the article said there were 72,197 centenarians in 2014, up from
50,281 in 2000. There were only 15,000 people over the
age of 100 in 1980.

Do you see a trend here, folks?

What those who analyze this data are further impressed with is that, not only are there more centenarians
around these days, but they are living even longer. The article pointed out that the data by the CDCP revealed that

"death rates declined for all demographic groups of centenarians—white, black, Hispanic, female, male—in the six years ending in 2014."

"Death rates for centenarian women dropped 14 percent in the six years ending in 2014, to 36.5 per 100 women, and by 20 percent to 33.2 per 100 men," the *Times* article stated.

Women, Tavernise pointed out, still outlive men, claiming more than 80 percent of the over-100 ranks. The writer anticipates that baby boomers just now entering retirement will bump up the numbers of the elderly in America to record levels and the rise in centenarians may just be the tip of the iceberg.

Interestingly, medical science still doesn't quite understand the massive needs for geriatric medicine and treatment protocols for the aging population. Is treating a 95-year-old with an orthopedic issue the same as treating a 50-year-old? Who is going to provide medical care for the older adults? We are facing a staggering shortage of physicians who will serve the aging population.

When I was in my caregiving role, I realized my mother was going to several doctors, each of whom specialized in a different area of medicine. She had her internist, who would refer her to a cardiologist and then to a rheumatoid specialist. After all of that, I would end up taking her to an endocrine specialist. I'm sure those doctors were well-trained in their chosen fields, but they did their own thing. When they recommended a treatment for what ailed my mother, it usually involved another prescription drug.

"Just take this and see me again in 30 days," was their mantra.

After a couple of years of this, it occurred to me that they were treating body systems, not her as an individual —a whole person.

I started asking questions. Why so many drugs? Were there alternatives, such as diet, for example, that could perhaps achieve the same medical goal? Was there anyone who could evaluate the big picture?

Apparently, medical specialists are reluctant to question others in their peer group. Maybe this is out of professional courtesy. I seemed to be raising these questions to no avail. It seemed to me that they expected older people like my mother to have poor health. I decided to be proactive about my mother's health. I searched for and found a medication manager. I was eager to see if my mother needed to be on 11 different prescriptions. What I learned was amazing (and infuriating). No. She did not need to be on that many medications. The out-of-pocket cost for all of these prescriptions was over $900 each month. And it was actually out of *my* pocket, which was my retirement fund.

After finding a doctor who practiced integrated medication management, we were able to take her off of three prescriptions, and her health gradually improved. After three months, we were able to get her off of two more. Down from 11 prescriptions to six. We saw a huge improvement in her physical health, and a big improvement in my financial health! A real win-win by being proactive with her care.

Here's the reality of the situation for the baby boomers: The Institute of Medicine released a report in 2009 called "Retooling for an Aging America: Building the Healthcare Workforce." The report said the demand for sophisticated geriatric care will increase dramatically as baby boomers age. And, if the trends continue, the number of board-certified geriatricians which, at the time of the survey, numbered around 7,000, will still be under 8,000 in 2030, when the real need to meet the aging population will reach 36,000. In the field of geriatric psychology, the shortage is even worse, with only 2,000 professionals available, and little prospect for any increases in the near future. The report revealed that only 1 percent of nurses are certified in geriatrics, and only 4 percent of social workers and 1 percent of physician assistants identify themselves as specializing in the field of geriatric medicine. So, older adults must be their own advocates to obtain the care they need.

Then there is this from James S. Marks, M.D., M.P.H., Director of the National Center for Chronic Disease Prevention and Health Promotion:

"Research has shown that poor health does not have to be an inevitable consequence of growing older. Death is inevitable, but, for many people, it need not be preceded by a slow, painful and disability-ridden decline. Our nation will continue to age that we cannot change—but we can delay and in many cases, prevent illness and disability."

The Alliance for Aging Research maintains that the aging population, as it changes, will stress the healthcare system because there will be a tendency to treat older individuals the same as younger people.

"In recent years, evidence has been mounting to suggest that, at all levels in the delivery of healthcare, there is a prevailing bias—ageism—that is at odds with the best interest of older people. This prejudice against the old in American healthcare is evidenced by scores of recent clinical studies, surveys and medical commentaries, many of which are referenced here. In this report, we outline five key dimensions of ageist bias in which U.S. healthcare fails older Americans:

- Health care professionals do not receive enough training in geriatrics to properly care for many older patients.

- Older patients are less likely than younger people to receive preventive care.

- Older patients are less likely to be tested or screened for diseases and other health problems.

- Proven medical interventions for older patients are often ignored, leading to inappropriate or incomplete treatment.

- Older people are consistently excluded from clinical trials, even though they are the largest users of approved drugs."
  (*Source: http://www.longtermcarelink.net/eldercare/medical_care_issues.htm*)

Old age is not a disease, and many medical problems are inappropriately attributed to old age. We need major transformation in the healthcare system with regard to shifting the medical paradigm to recognize that treatment of the 90-plus population requires as thoughtful consideration for root-cause diagnosis as treatment of a 40-year-old. The fact that age is rising does not imply you must default to sickness and disease and "just accept it." I don't know about you, but as soon as a doctor starts the dialogue with "At your age ..." it's time to find a caring, experienced geriatric medical practitioner.

CHAPTER VII

WHEN IS THE RIGHT TIME TO MOVE INTO RETIREMENT COMMUNITIES?

A CCRC (CONTINUING CARE RETIREMENT COMMUNITY) is an alternative residence choice for older adults (usually 55–65 and older) that can provide flexible housing options combined with an array of services that can address changing health and wellness needs as its residents age. The idea behind this growing trend is to make it possible for residents to move in and never have to move again. If their needs change, and they require healthcare and supervision they do not have to leave friends, or their spouse, behind. They avoid the stress of another move. They are able to receive the healthcare they need for as long as they need it.

But when is the right time to make the move? There are many considerations in choosing the right CCRC for you. Involved are lifestyle, finances, your individual housing preference, healthcare options and your future happiness. So you don't want to make an uninformed decision.

First, not all CCRCs are created equal. You will be required to sign a contract. If you check on the contracts offered by CCRCs across America, you will find that there are many different types of contracts. It is impossible to be thoroughly acquainted with every nuance of each of them, but it is possible to determine what you need and want and work from there. If you own long-term-care insurance, you will want to make sure that your coverage harmonizes with what you select. That's a major financial consideration.

Does the CCRC require an entry fee? A growing number are now offering rental contracts. What are the terms? Does the contract allow you to recoup any of the entry fee after the first few years? Some CCRCs offer "return-of-capital" contracts where part of the entry fee will be refunded if the resident dies or moves. But ROC contracts may have a higher entry fee, so you just must read the fine print, or have someone you trust do it.

How stable is the community, financially? Can it fulfill its long-term commitment to provide you with adequate healthcare? How long have they been operating? How experienced is the CCRC's management? Will they be able to offer you the type of care you need and expect? Ask about ratings. Check on complaints. What is the staff turnover record?

The reason I mention all this "homework" is because I have seen decisions made hastily that some of my clients have come to regret. Remember the housing downturn that began in 2007 and lasted through 2009? Many CCRC occupancy rates dropped. Why? Because prospective residents couldn't find buyers for their homes. This had a domino effect and some CCRCs even went bankrupt.

What about state regulations? Does your state have a regulatory agency? In Florida, the continuing care industry is regulated under Chapter 651 of the Florida Statutes. It all falls under the regulatory umbrella of the Florida Department of Financial Services (formerly the Florida

Department of Insurance). The Agency for Health Care Administration (AHCA) oversees the nursing aspects of assisted living and nursing home facilities in the Sunshine State. The Department of Elder Affairs (DOEA) is involved with policies and procedures.

Those agencies and organizations are your tax dollars at work, and it is comforting to know they are there, but the ball is in your court when making the choice of where you want to live.

FEE INCREASES

One of the most common sources of complaints among CCRC residents is when fees are increased. When you are living on a fixed income, that can be painful to the pocket book. An increase of 4-6 percent is not uncommon, according to Kiplinger's. It may be wise to check recent annual reports of the CCRC. Are rate hikes spelled out in the contract? What has been the history of rate increases at the facility you are considering? The Kiplinger's article also stated that "facilities may attempt to discharge residents if they run out of money or develop above-average care needs." It advised seniors to check for specific circumstances that might justify the facility forcing out a resident. "Look out for fuzzy language, such as involuntary discharges being allowed for 'good cause,'" said Eric Carson, directing attorney at the National Senior Citizen's Law Center, who was quoted in the article. (*Source: www.kiplinger.com/article/retirement/T037-C000-S000-risks-and-rewards-of-moving-to-a-ccrc.*)

Can you negotiate with CCRCs before you sign the dotted line? Perhaps you can. Some of them are eager to fill empty apartments. You may be able to pay a portion of the entrance fee now and the rest later. You may also negotiate a refund of the fee if you change your mind and move.

Contracts are agreements between two parties. You are one of the parties.

TRANSITIONING CARE

You could begin your residency at a community at one level of care, or none at all, and, down the road, require a different level of care.

"Residents may feel pressured to move from one level of care to another," said the Kiplinger's article, "such as when a facility says it cannot deliver the required care in an independent-living unit. That may mean leaving a long-time home in the independent-living unit and being separated from a spouse—resulting in higher fees for a couple occupying two units. Some CCRCs have an appeals process for residents who are transferred involuntarily."

The article pointed out the wisdom of asking about these things before signing. Push to have your own physician involved in the decision. Could you hire your own care providers in addition to those who work for the CCRC? To get a true feel for what life is like at the CCRC you are considering, why not drop in unannounced a few times? Have a meal. Talk to individuals and ask them what they think of the place. What kinds of activities are available? How do they get along with the staff and management there? Ask someone you trust what they observe. This type of advance inspection can save heartache later.

Roger Stevens, CEO of Westminster Retirement Communities of Florida, was an excellent resource for me in researching this subject. He is a nationally recognized speaker and thought-leader on retirement care communities and has been in the continuing care industry for more than 30 years.

He realizes the decision to move into a CCRC is an emotional one.

"Once you pay, you're in," he says. "You will be taken care of the rest of your life. But it is a big decision."

Stevens recommends checking the CCRC's Fitch Rating, bond rating and credit rating.

"The best predictor of the future is the past," he says.

According to the Zeigler National CCRC Listing and Profile, more than half of all continuing care retirement communities are faith-based. Among those affiliations, 21.1 percent are Lutheran, 17.6 percent are Methodist, 13.8 percent are Presbyterian, and 12.8 are Roman Catholic.

Because Roger is a national thought-leader, I wanted to tap into his expertise in identifying how to have the discussion with your loved ones about transitioning to a life-care community.

"What's interesting is that the label, 'Continuing Care Retirement Community' is changing," says Roger. I probed to learn more, and he essentially explained that we're seeing a transition to life care communities. I asked how to open the discussion and he stressed there was no one model, or single approach. It's all based on the circumstances of the older adults, and the children. Moving into a life-care community needs to be based on the wants and desires of prospective residents, he said. For example, if the focus is on healthcare, that would be one type of evaluation. Whereas, if the focus is on lifestyle, that would suggest a different culture within a community.

Here are some ideas he shares if you are considering this type of lifestyle for yourself or your family member:

- Read the contracts, understand them, discuss them, and meet with residents in the community; remember when you sign the contract, it's for life.

- Determine the financial strength of the organization you're signing the contract with.

- Get a history of monthly fee adjustments, and determine how the history compares with COLA adjustments going back 10 years.

- If the community is a continuing care community with assisted living and skilled nursing care, what's the quality of care?

- Look at state surveys and other regulatory examinations.

- Talk to people who live there, eat lunch and dinner there. Get feedback and visit a lot.

- Make sure you know what's important to you.

- Walk through the communities to get over the perception, it's a nursing home; it's an active living community and you need to experience it.

- Ask to get a copy of the monthly newsletter. This tells you a lot about the community.

When you are engaging family members in the "is it time to move?" dialogue, Roger offers the following resource materials that may be helpful:

- *How to Best Communicate to Senior Adults* by David Solie

- *Being Mortal* by Atul Garwande

- *Hard Choices for Loving People* by Hank Dunn

Roger also offers suggestions to those helping family members evaluate what is best for their health and well-being.

"Determine what your loved one wants, not what you want for them," he says. He encourages people to clearly understand the difference between for-profit communities and nonprofit communities. A key question to ask when evaluating a community is "what happens if Mom runs out of money?" Typically, in a for-profit setting, Mom will have to exit. But, in a nonprofit, Mom's care is paid for life because typically, nonprofit communities have foundations that help with additional funding.

Since I had the opportunity to spend some quality discussion time with Roger, I wanted to know what his experience has been regarding the quality of life for those in life-care communities, versus facilities where residents live independently and with perhaps higher degrees of isolation. His response was passionate.

"There is no better day than a day spent with residents," he said. He loves the residents because they have so much history, and all residents have the three critical components of total well-being in a life-care community: great nutrition, great health care and great socialization.

According to Roger, one of the drawbacks of this type of community lifestyle is that the majority of facilities are for upper-middle-income and upper-income people. Westminster focuses on middle-income and slightly-below-middle-income individuals. Roger has a think tank group he meets with regularly, the Leading Age National Association. Not only are they trying to come up with a different name to remove the perception that these communities are "nursing homes," but they are attempting to figure out strategies to help individuals understand that life-care communities are not just for the affluent.

"There are some very affordable solutions, and affordable communities out there," he said.

ALTERNATIVE HOUSING OPTIONS FOR LONG-TERM CARE

Options for long-term care were once very limited when considering independent, assisted and nursing home living. Research indicates that 90 percent of individuals prefer to stay home as they age. I know from personal experience that was the way it was going to be with my caregiving roles. But, to accommodate my families' "aging in place" needs, it required a room addition, along with a lot of other services and support to ensure quality of life and quality of care. So, the decision to age in place needs thorough and thoughtful analysis. It is not to be underestimated in terms of commitment, cost and, most importantly, quality of personal care—both emotional, and physical.

Trends evolving in communities throughout the United States are providing alternative housing arrangements. It's become evident that public policy leaders cannot talk about public health issues without considering deeply the impact baby boomers are going to have on demands for skilled nursing care. One of the earliest innovations is what is called "naturally occurring retirement communities, or NORCs, which cater to those who don't want to leave their home or community as they age. These types of communities focus on continuous growth of the individual, making life for the aging adult more pleasurable and healthy, rather than focusing on declining health and well-being.

I had the privilege of learning from one individual, Barbara Tidwell, who wanted to make a difference in the lives of older adults who need skilled nursing care. Here's her story, which is ever so inspiring due to her commitment and passion to create a quality home environment for the residents she cares for with her caregivers.

BARBARA TIDWELL
OWNER, FOUNDER OF SOME PLACE LIKE HOME

Barbara Tidwell is owner and founder of Some Place Like Home, Inc., which has developed into a refreshing alternative to nursing homes. The mission of SPLH is to provide professional quality healthcare services to senior citizens in a home-like setting. It has been described as a "bed and breakfast" concept for senior care.

When Barbara was a young girl, she developed a deep love for older people. She was raised by her grandparents in eastern Kentucky. As she grew older, her dream was to provide a place where she could return the love that her grandparents had shown for her, by giving older people a safe, caring home in their later years.

"I was a coal-miner's daughter," she said. "In fact, one of my cousins married one of Loretta Lynn's cousins."

Barbara said her grandparents raised 12 kids, and her grandmother was 90 years old when Barbara knew her.

"They didn't believe in wasting anything," Barbara said. "When I outgrew my clothes, my grandmother would make me new ones—out of feed sacks. I never thought of us as poor. We had a large extended family with a lot of love."

Today, Barbara is a registered dietician and teaches nutrition and long-term-care administration at the University of North Florida in Jacksonville. She is a fellow in the American College of Healthcare Executives with more than 45 years' experience in the healthcare field. She is also an exercise specialist.

Barbara Tidwell

She moved to Jacksonville from Hopkinsville, Kentucky, in 1980 and built a hotel-style restaurant and designed a kitchen for St. Luke's Hospital. She started Some Place Like Home in 1998.

"I wanted to have a home for elderly people that would feel, to them, like home," she said. "When I retired from St. Luke's Hospital, I took my pension and invested in homes that would have room for six residents. That way we wouldn't have to have the property rezoned. My husband sold his company and invested in SPLH. I suppose you could say it is a cross between assisted living and a nursing care facility."

"We have a one-to-two staff ratio," she continued. "Forty-seven employees taking care of 24 people. The cost is between $7,000 and $7,500 per month, but that is all-inclusive. When they need to visit the doctor's office, we take them. Depending on their ability to get around, we take our residents on very enjoyable excursion trips."

Barbara says that games, entertainment, parties and field trips keep life fun and interesting for residents.

Barbara admits that many SPLH residents are wealthy. Many SPLH applicants come from retirement communities like Sunrise of Jacksonville and Vicar's Landing in Ponte Vedra.

I asked Barbara, what saddens her the most?

"The loneliness and isolation that some of the older ones feel," she said. "A lot have families who are so busy they can't stay long when they visit them. And they don't seem to have a lot in common.

"We teach our staff how to keep engaged with the residents," she continued. "Think of fun stuff."

She said she tries to keep staff members who are 40 years and older so they can relate better to older people.

"Kids sometimes paint a picture of their parents in their minds, but they don't really see them," said Barbara. "They need to take the blinders off and really know them, so they can take care of them better when the time comes."

Barbara says that when her parents were older, she had to take them in. Her method of caring for them was to bring in home healthcare, not to drag the parents out of their homes.

"We allow our people to bring their animals with them when they come to Some Place Like Home," she says. "It helps create the comfortable atmosphere that goes with a peaceful home."

Barbara's example is one that is working well. She has a goal to create more homes that will give older adults who can no longer care for themselves an intimate, more pleasurable lifestyle. In an article entitled, "Alternative Housing Options for Long-Term Care," AARP said the Eden Alternative "focuses on changing the atmosphere and experience found in long-term care facilities."

The Eden Alternative is a not-for-profit organization with 300 registered homes in the United States, Canada, Europe and Australia.

GREEN HOUSE PROJECT

Another similar project is the Green House Project, which caters to the entire life of older adults, not just their healthcare needs. According to AARP, the idea behind this project is "to provide your loved ones with quality of life enriched by relationships with qualified staff who choose to work in an environment focused on enriching the life of the older adult."

The AARP comments on the warmth and happiness in Green House facilities. "No sterile environment here," the article stated, adding that the facilities are focused on community, relationships, well-being and happiness. AARP says Green House facilities typically house between six and 10 residents per home, and each resident has a private room and custom-decorated bathrooms, much like Barbara's homes. AARP says there are over 50 Green Houses in the U.S., and reports indicated that more than 100 are in development, thanks to funding by the Robert Wood Johnson Foundation.

OTHER "AGING IN PLACE" COMMUNITIES

Other similar "aging in place" communities are prevalent in Boston's Beacon Hill Village, which caters to those who want to stay in their own home for as long as possible. Then there's Capitol Hill Village, a nonprofit membership organization in the heart of our nation's capital, which offers typical retirement home services in an in-home setting for the members. It was started by a group of local retirees. They provide a network of services to individuals desiring to continue living in their own homes as long as possible. The idea is to help older adults take charge of their future and stay at home with supportive resources. How innovative! I believe we will see many more creative approaches to senior living as the population ages.

The Jewish Federations of North America (JFNA) has had an impactful role on naturally occurring retirement communities, as well as facilitating the development of Community Innovations for Aging in Place (CIAIP). This organization developed these types of residential models for older adults more than 25 years ago. Federation leaders brought the model to the attention of Congress, and were able to get 26 states to create demonstration projects. These projects organize and locate a range of coordinated health care, social services and group activities on site. They create strong communities partnerships that unite housing entities and residents, health and social service providers, government agencies, and philanthropic organizations.

The JFNA has also launched the NORC (Naturally Occurring Retirement Communities) Aging In Place initiative whose role is to:

- Promote independence and healthy aging by engaging seniors before a crisis and respond to their changing needs over time
- Provide seniors with vital roles in the development and operation of these programs
- Fill the gaps where Medicare, Medicaid, or Older Americans Act services are insufficient or inadequately coordinated but not to duplicate them.

(*Source:www.aarp.org/relationships/caregiving-resource-center/info-10-2010/ho_alternative_housing_options_for_long_term_care.html*)

Innovative aging-in-place strategies like these will allow older adults to live in dignity and optimize their emotional, mental, physical and spiritual well-being. I had the opportunity to interview several caregivers to gather their perspective on their role as a caregiver because they chose to have their loved ones "age in place." Their insights are shared in the next chapter.

CHAPTER VIII

INSIGHTS FROM CAREGIVERS

I HAVE A SPECIAL PLACE IN MY HEART for caregivers, having been one for most of my adult life. When a family member is in need, caregivers respond. It's just what they do, reflexively, without thinking. Just the same as one would help a stranger who was drowning, or a friend who lost a loved one, caregivers don't complain or whine or make excuses, they just roll up their sleeves and go. They know it's a thankless role, yet they do it with a spirit of gratitude for being chosen for this ever so important role in life. They do what needs to be done—as long as they are needed—whether it is for a spouse, a sibling, a parent or grandparent. Anyone they consider family. Caregivers seldom take a holiday. Few will be recognized publicly for what they do. Their reward is the inner feeling of satisfaction of knowing they have done their duty for kith and kin.

According to estimates from the National Alliance for Caregiving, during the past year, 65.7 million Americans (or 29 percent of the adult U.S. adult population, involving 31 percent of all U.S. households) served as family caregivers for an ill or disabled relative. One of the fastest-growing segments of the U.S. population is that of older caregivers. According to the NAC, the typical "older adult" caregiver is a 79-year-old white female currently caring for one adult (spouse, child or sibling), who needs care because of a long-term physical condition. She has been providing this care for, on average, more than five years and spends an average of 34 hours a week helping a loved one with 1.5 ADLs (activities of daily living) or nursing tasks. She is usually the sole provider of such care and is unpaid. She is typically married and her average household income is just over $50,000. (*Source: http:// www.caregiving.org/wp-content/uploads/2015/05/Caregiving-in-the-US-2015_75orOlder_CGProfile.pdf*)

Family Caregivers

2 out of 5 adults are CAREGIVERS

60% of caregivers are women

The typical caregiver is 49, female, taking care of her widowed mother, and juggling her career and family.

70% of caregivers make adjustments to work schedules to accommodate caregiving responsibilities.

On average, women caregivers lose **$324,044** in lost wages, social security benefits, and retirement plans over a lifetime.

Caregivers' estimated out-of-pocket costs: **$5,531** annually

Women caregivers are **2x** more likely than non-caregivers to end up in poverty

Each year caregivers provide **$470 billion** worth of unpaid care.

Learn more at:
Women's Institute for a Secure Retirement
wiserwomen.org

WISER
WOMEN'S INSTITUTE FOR A SECURE RETIREMENT

Source: http://www.wiserwomen.org/?id=96

Other reports from AARP provide the following compelling data on the growth of caregiving in the United States:

People who care for adult family members or friends fulfill an important role, not only for the people they assist, but for society as a whole. While this care is unpaid, its value has been estimated at $257 billion annually. Although caregivers make many contributions, being a caregiver may take a personal toll.

The AARP study was based on a national survey of 6,139 adults, from which 1,247 caregivers were identified. Caregivers are defined as 18 years of age or older, living in the United States, and providing one or more activities of daily living (ADLs), or instrumental ADLs (IADLs) for someone aged 18 or older.

Key findings include:

- There are an estimated 44.4 million caregivers in the United States who, on average, provide 21 hours of care per week. The average length of caregiving is 4.3 years.

- Many caregivers fulfill multiple roles. Most caregivers are married or living with a partner (62 percent), and most have worked and managed caregiving responsibilities at the same time (59 percent).

- The typical caregiver is a 46-year-old woman who has at least some college experience and provides more than 20 hours of care each week to her mother.

- Male caregivers are more likely to be working full-time (60 percent) than female caregivers (41 percent), and female caregivers are more likely to be working part-time (14 percent) than male caregivers.

- The most frequently reported unmet needs of caregivers are finding time for oneself (35 percent), managing emotional and physical stress (29 percent) and balancing work and family responsibilities (29 percent).

What follows are interviews with caregivers who were willing to share with me what keeps them going and their view of life in the retirement years.

Kathy Glasser, Caregiver to husband

Kathy has been a caregiver since 2008 to her husband, Jeff, who had a severe stroke in February of that year. Jeff went to therapy for four years, and after they had done all they could do for him, the rest was up to Kathy.

Kathy worked at Walt Disney World and retired in her late 40s. She had planned on working longer, but Jeff's stroke changed everything. Kathy has had her own share of health problems. In 2006, when her daughter was 10 years old, Kathy was diagnosed with breast cancer, but is doing well now, having responded to treatment.

Kathy says that prayer and staying focused and proactive are her best bulwarks against negativity. She told me that she has sought and received help from a therapist whose coaching has helped her greatly.

"Jeff can't walk or talk, and he can't stand up," Kathy said. "Other than that he is healthy. He has a good heart, but he cannot do anything on his own

"What do you do for yourself?" I asked.

"I ride my bicycle and work in the yard," Kathy said, adding that she enjoys eating out with friends when she can. She will occasionally get a break when one of her friends agrees to look after Jeff while she takes in a movie. Even then, she calls every hour or so to make sure everything is OK. This is typical of a caregiver's internal pressure. You can get away physically, but emotionally and mentally, you can never get away from the caregiving responsibility.

"I want people to know that I enjoy spending time with my husband," Kathy says. "He is a fighter, and has not given up. We use the iPad to communicate with each other. We have date night every night, with wine, and I set him up in a room that has all of his things from the past. He always reaches up for hugs and kisses when he sees me."

Kathy says that a highlight of Jeff's day is when his guy friends come from church to see him.

"We keep a refrigerator in his room and he has a milkshake every day at 4 p.m.—something he looks forward to," she said.

What advice would you give to other caregivers?" I asked.

"Ask lots of questions," Kathy said. "Don't settle for what one person says is the answer to any physical condition they exhibit. Be an advocate for them and be persistent in that advocacy. Take care of yourself. Find new ways to love your partner. Embrace the challenge and feel God's compassion for you."

Kathy says that, despite the sadness that accompanies illness, she has found different ways to appreciate her husband. She admires the way his bravery is an example to others. She relies on her "support system," consisting of her eight brothers and sisters. Her devotion and commitment to finding ways to continue her love journey with her husband is beyond inspiring. In our Skype visit, she insisted I meet Jeff. She turned the camera to him only to introduce me to a man who illuminated the room with joy, despite his physical challenges. This demonstrated the impact Kathy has had on his life through her unconditional commitment to making his life comfortable.

Kathy has had to set her career, her personal needs and her aspirations aside to assume this most important role. She stays focused on what she needs to do for Jeff, and still creates opportunities to be a mother, a wife, a woman and a caregiver. She made the personal choice to keep him at home rather than in a skilled nursing facility. So, for Kathy, retirement is essentially a full-time job as a caregiver. She does have things that make her sad, but she is clear that they don't make her angry, just sad. Things such as Jeff not being able to walk her daughter down the aisle. Not being able to go to University of Florida Gator games and not traveling with Jeff. She has had to move on with living her life, and says that living with Jeff is still a part of her life. She has to work hard to maintain her stamina by taking naps, praying, giving herself permission to do things that she feels like doing when she needs to do them, such as exercise, reading and, of most importance, her strong faith walk. She says Jeff allows her to do the things she needs to do.

ANN JUNOD, CAREGIVER TO HUSBAND, MOTHER AND FATHER
Another inspiration is Ann Junod. She has devoted her life to the care of others. Her most recent charge, her father, Olen Lovell, Jr., whose story appears elsewhere in this book, died in early 2016. Ann also cared for her now-deceased husband, Robert Junod.

Ann and Robert met at the Atlanta Golf Classic in 1977 through mutual friends and were married the next year. Robert was in sales at the time, a job which required a lot of travel. Shortly before they married, Robert's car was struck from behind by another automobile while he was on a business trip in Chicago, Illinois. That accident marked the start of his back problems that, over the years, put him in the hospital for epidurals and traction treatment. He finally submitted to back surgery in 2002. In addition to his back ailments, in the 1980s, Robert dealt with lymphoma, a type of cancer which required him to have radiation and chemotherapy. He dealt with this disease twice—the first time they gave him radiation treatments, the second time radiation and chemo.

Ann retired in 1999 at the age of 51 after teaching elementary school for 30 years in the suburbs of Atlanta. They bought a home in Palm Coast, just south of St. Augustine. She and her husband became involved in volunteer work. Ann chose the public school system and Robert chose the police department.

In 2000, her father had back surgery, which did not go well. Her mother couldn't care for him because she had macular degeneration, so the task fell to Ann to stay with him while he was bedridden. Even afterward, she frequently made the 30-minute drive from Palm Coast to St. Augustine to care for their daily needs and taking them to the doctor. Her mother died in 2002 from a heart attack, and her father died at age 99 on Feb. 26, 2016.

"I had great support from my stepson and daughter-in-law," Ann says. "They stepped in so I could travel back and forth to Tampa to visit my brother." Her brother was in a skilled nursing facility in Tampa, Florida, after suffering a heart attack. "I also have great friends and neighbors," Ann said.

The breaks from her caregiving responsibilities have helped Ann to persevere.

"I have traveled to Europe on several occasions," said Ann. "I have a friend in Atlanta who takes in foreign exchange students. Over the years, I have gotten to know them and have enjoyed attending two weddings in Germany and one in Poland where we stayed in a palace."

Ann walks almost every morning.

"I take care of myself," Ann says. "I stay busy volunteering for several organizations. I was recently ordained as a deacon in my church, which is a big part of my life."

Ann misses her parents, who she says were always so giving that it made caring for them a labor of love.

"To know them was to love them," she said.

Ann offers this caregiver's advice:

- Give yourself permission to travel because this will serve as a recovery getaway.

- Exercise, take care of yourself.

- Make sure you have a group of good friends as part of your support system

- Keep friends who listen and understand and don't put unreasonable expectations on you.

- Stay active with your church family and make friends from your church as this becomes a good resource pool for you.

- Take care of yourself mentally, physically and spiritually.

I wanted to get a final gold nugget from Ann about what she perceives as a key value of her caregiving role, and she was quick to respond, "Why, of course, it's honor and respect."

Doesn't that sum it up? Caregivers simply walk the talk by honoring and respecting those who are entrusted in their loving care.

ON A PERSONAL NOTE

I could not end this chapter without sharing my personal insights on the caregiving role, since I was blessed to be a caregiver to my mother and great aunt for 33 years. Yes, 33 years.

My mother lived to 93 and had neither financial resources nor adequate long-term care insurance to provide quality care. So, I chose to provide the care in my home, although it was a decision I made without knowing the consequences.

Then, I cared for an elderly great-aunt who had no children and no roof over her head. She lived just over age 100. I reasoned that, had my father been alive, he would have taken care of them, so I viewed it as my family duty and obligation.

Does a caregiver do everything right and stay pure to the role? Absolutely not! We are human. We operate with human emotions. I had plenty of time to experience every emotion known to mankind. I want to say to all caregivers out there that it is normal to sometimes operate in anger, fear, frustration, guilt, denial, confusion, isolation, and the list goes on.

I am a "type A" personality. I didn't take the advice that Kathy Glasser and Ann Junod offered in their stories. I never gave myself permission to "get away and recharge." Caregivers create behaviors and approaches that are unique to the situation in which they find themselves. I did not heed the advice of Kathy and Ann to "take care of myself." I felt I had to be super human. I convinced myself I could do it all, and be all things to all people. I felt I had to be at every doctor's appointment, to single-handedly take care of every need of those in my care, to maintain my home, and, at the same time, to manage my career. After all, I had to make the money to pay for help when I was working or travelling on business. So, I did what you *should not do* as a caregiver. I did not take advantage of outside resources. As far as I was concerned, they didn't exist.

The world of caregiving 10 to 15 years ago is quite different than it is today. These days there are many organizations that support caregivers.

With the aging population in America, caregiving is taking a toll on the nation's baby boomers, who are caring for aging parents. Women are at significant risk. Ultimately, this impacts financial security for baby boomers, as they find themselves scaling back on their careers, as Kathy had to. Or they are taking on caregiving responsibilities, as Ann did, and postponing their dream retirement.

The stress of being a caregiver is impacting one out of four U.S. households, according to the American Society on Aging. Forty percent of caregivers are also raising children just the situation in which Kathy found herself. These types of long-term commitments can exact a physical and emotional toll— whether you admit it or not. The toll can also be financial, per the National Center on Women and Aging. The NCWA found that, on average, caregivers lose $659,130 over their lifetimes in reduced salary and retirement benefits.

It's easy for caregivers to forget about their own needs, as I did. So, here are some commonly offered support tips:

- Come to terms with and accept your own limitations. You don't have to do it all. Get help when you feel overwhelmed.

- Create a caregiver support team. Have resources lined up. Make a list of people you can trust. Plan ahead.

- Create a system. If you have other responsibilities and commitments (children, career), stay organized. It will help you manage stress and maintain your own health and well-being.

- Schedule time for yourself and the activities you enjoy—you need to stay healthy in mind, body and spirit.

- Make your own health as important a priority as the health of those in your care. Eat a balanced diet, get plenty of rest, and exercise regularly.

- Find ways to relieve stress through relaxation techniques that work for you. Establish a routine and commit to it. It could be spiritual exercises, spiritual direction, meditation, prayer, yoga—whatever works for you.

- Get regular physical, emotional and financial checkups to make sure everything is on track.

Caregiving is a genuinely tough job. It requires an entire infrastructure of support, so don't go at it alone. I have to say that from my own personal experience, it is one of the most rewarding life-defining experiences you can ever have. It will define who you will be for the rest of your life, and provide you with experiences and memories that will last your lifetime.

CHAPTER IX

SIMPLIFYING YOUR LIFE AND LETTING GO OF THINGS!

BEFORE WRITING THIS CHAPTER, I was struggling trying to figure out how to address something no one wants to talk about, and that's how to begin letting go of all your worldly possessions as you get into your very senior years (and I mean into your upper 90s and 100s).

Our human inclination is to hold onto things that, for whatever reason, have become attachments in our lives. We tend to cling to things as if they were attached to us like our arms and legs. But do we really want our loved ones discarding our possessions after we slip the surly bonds of earth and depart this life?

Over the years, I have worked with many of the heirs of my clients, and I have seen a pattern develop. The loved ones we leave behind tend to experience emotional turmoil when faced with the task of closing their deceased parents' home and disposing of their material possessions. These things, while they meant a lot to their parents, may not have the same sentimental value to them. We need to ask ourselves, do we want to put our children or grandchildren in this situation? I have been there. Allow me to share a story with you that will illustrate why it is better to let your worldly possessions go while you are still alive.

MY FRIEND, PAT

My precious friend and client, Pat O'Neill, passed away on Easter Sunday in 2015. She came into my life right after her husband had died in August 2007. I had just changed jobs. I had left the corporate world and was working for a company that I would purchase a few years later. Pat was one of the reasons I founded Woman's Worth®, a company that specializes in helping women and their unique financial needs.

The then-owner of the company I worked for said he needed help with a certain widow who had no idea of how to manage her financial affairs because she was used to her husband doing everything for her. All she had done was work and save money. The couple had no children and no family on either side. When Pat's husband died, she was on her own and left to fend for herself in a financial world that did not speak her language.

Pat O'Neill with the author

Because Pat was perceived by the owner of the company to be so in need of help that went beyond the professional pale, he asked me if I would do what I could for her. Being the bleeding heart I am, I agreed to help her get organized. I had no idea what I was taking on. This, I soon discovered, was going to be a major project. Pat had no inkling of what her financial position was. She didn't even know how to write checks, let alone balance a checkbook. She could have been taken advantage of very easily by a con artist or a slick salesman.

I went to work getting her organized. I set up financial systems for her and established controls. I would swing by Pat's home every six weeks or so and help her sort through her mail. I kept her checking account balanced, and made sure she had the cash she needed to take care of her basic needs. Our relationship became more than just client and advisor. She needed all manner of personal attention and compassion. I had to step way outside the professional box and … just be there for her.

Remember, she had a large estate that she really didn't know she had. Pat had no children, no family members, no heirs. She didn't care about money. She lived like she was poor, and had virtually every possession she had ever owned, including clothes from her high school days. It occurred to me that the reason for her hoarding mindset was because she had lived through the Great Depression of the 1930s. For her to throw out anything, including scraps of food and worn-out clothing, was, to her, a wasteful act. She had a three-bedroom, two-bath home with a three-car garage. The garage was stacked with cast-off furniture, old clothes, books, and all kinds of items she no longer used or had a use for. Even the storage area behind the garage was overflowing with stuff.

Pat was 79 years old when I met her, and I believe it was a divine blessing. Her birthday is the same day as my mother's passing. In my mind, God replaced my caregiving role for my mother and handed me another caregiving responsibility. As time passed, I was to realize that I felt that same warm glow of satisfaction helping this woman, who was of no blood relation to me, as I did helping my mother. I found myself not only navigating her through the financial system, the health care system and the emotional swings that any octogenarian would face growing older, but also dealing with physical setbacks of her failing health. She was growing ever frailer and needed help, and I was there to provide it.

Through the years, I learned a lot about her. She told me how her mother had sent her off to boarding school at the tender age of 7, and how she had never had a real birthday party. The closest thing to it was when her aunt one day brought her a slice of cake on her birthday. I reflected on how much we don't know about other people until we ask. I couldn't imagine what it was like not having family. In lieu of blood kin, I became her family, so to speak. I gave her moral support, spiritual advice, and protected her estate.

I decided that I would arrange for Pat to have an 80th birthday party. After all, it is a major milestone in a person's life. We picked her favorite restaurant and invited 16 of her friends from the gym where she went each day to swim. We decorated a private room in the restaurant with flowers and balloons. The look on her face when she figured out what was going on was priceless. She cried her way through the entire affair. She sobbed when she saw her birthday cake.

After I had Pat safely back home and was driving to my own house, I reflected on the fact that I was the luckiest one to have someone like her in my life. And lucky even more because I am privileged to be able to hear the stories of the other "Pats" of the world, whose stories are there but for the asking.

I know before I say this that it may sound morbid, but toward the end of Pat's life, I encouraged her to complete a death journal of what she wanted to have done with all her things and what charities we needed to focus on when she passed away. When she died at age 87, there was a lot of stuff that had to be dealt with, and I was to be the one to deal with it. The official trustee of her estate was a local attorney, and I had a feeling that he was not about to spend the time it would take to close down her homestead and deal with all of Pat's personal possessions. I was right. He resigned from his role as soon as I notified him that she had passed away. The ball was thrown right back into my court.

Before she died, I had made a commitment to Pat to see that things would be cared for in the way she wished. The easy part was distributing the estate through the trust and the will, and funding her charitable foundation. That was a walk in the park compared to disposing of her clothes, furniture, electronics, jewelry, books, family portraits, artwork, pets and other personal items. I prayed my way through packing up Pat's home. I had been trying for seven years to get her to downsize and eliminate things she didn't need.

"Let's give things away to charities, or needy families," I suggested.

She would agree, but then, when it came time to let go, she just couldn't. She told me that, after she died, I could sell all her things and donate the proceeds to Mother Teresa's Sisters of Charity order. I tried to explain to her that things could not be so easily sold, and reminded her about the many garage sales she held that generated little cash and mostly headaches and back pain.

A few days after her funeral, I found myself packing her things into boxes and contacting Habitat for Humanity and the Salvation Army to come and take them. I experienced emotions that I had never felt. All these things represented her life. What was I to do with such things as family portraits, pictures of her wedding, and other items that represented her history? Throw them away? She had no family except a lone step-brother. He had no interest in them, although he was interested in who would get her estate.

I reflected on the fact that this is the pain and anguish that every family goes through in similar situations. I didn't experience this with my mother because she lived with me and had nothing but jewelry. One Christmas, I suggested that she pull out all her jewelry and have her daughters and granddaughters identify what pieces they wanted when she passed. My mother just gave the pieces to them. She had no need of them, she said. But Pat was different. So I cried my way through giving away the following:

- A house full of furniture and electronics
- 28 30-gallon bags of clothes
- 6 large moving boxes of shoes
- 3 large moving boxes of miscellaneous clothing
- More costume jewelry than can be counted
- Her precious cat, Sonny
- A piano
- Artwork from her very talented aunt
- Family portraits and family pictures

- 5 large construction bins full of things that were so old they could not even be given to charities.

I prayed I had made the right decisions.

Do you want your family to go through that? There are strategies that can help you, or your parents or grandparents, in the "letting go" process.

Joshua Fields Millburn in his blogs on the minimalist website, www.themimimalists.com, offers the following great advice:

> *"A sunset is beautiful, but it lasts only so long. Once it's over, it's over.*
>
> *"In time, perfection is tainted by life's beautiful blemishes, and every perfectionist dies a thousand deaths. We often look at the things we enjoy—the relationships, the experiences, the possessions—and we want to hold on to them forever. We expect that these things will continue to add the same value to our lives, day in and day out.*
>
> *"But life does not work this way. Not everything that adds value today will add value tomorrow.*
>
> *"This is particularly evident within our material possessions. Each time we purchase a sparkling new thingamabob, we bask in the light of its potential, excited by the initial value the new object brings to our lives. Over time, though, the value wanes, the glossy newness wears off, and our excitement abruptly dissipates.*
>
> *"When that possession stops adding value, however, what do we do? Do we ask ourselves why? Do we*

donate it or sell it or question why we purchased it in the first place? Not usually.

"Often, once the dullness sets in, we let our effects gather dust or wither away in boxes in our basements, closets, and junk drawers. Out of sight, out of mind.

"And but then the only way to reclaim the missing value is to find another thingamajig that is shiny and exciting and new. This cycle is a dangerous downward spiral, a vortex of consumption in which we're constantly looking for that next nugget of excitement, that next burst of euphoria, that cocaine high that doesn't last but a few feet past the cash register.

"Thankfully, there are at least two ways to break this vicious cycle.

"First, we must question our new purchases. Of course there's nothing inherently wrong with material possessions. What's wrong is the idea that material possessions will bring lasting joy and contentment. They won't. Instead, we must ask, Will this thing add value to my life? and Is this thing still adding value to my life? This kind of intentional living, when done consistently, will form lasting, empowering habits.

"Second, we must be willing to let go. We should let go of superfluous excess in our lives, starting with the dusty belongings inhabiting every nook and cranny and dark corner of our homes, eventually moving on to the more difficult things no longer adding value to our lives: sentimental items, unnecessarily large homes, the American Dream, extra cars, shitty relationships.

"Ultimately, we must learn to let go. To do so, acceptance is the key. We needn't settle, but we all have a reality we must accept. As much as we might want to, we'll never be able to hold on to a sunset. Likewise, we

can't retain every thing and still lead meaningful lives.
Life is fulfilling only when we allow ourselves to let go,
when we allow ourselves to be in the moment, when
we allow ourselves to feel the moment. After all, this
moment is life's only true reality."

I could not find better words to express the message
to let go of possessions. Thanks to Pat, and the lessons
learned from my mother's transitional journey to be with
the Lord, I, too, am a minimalist. Here are things I offer
you to consider:

- If you purchase new clothing—let's say you bought
two new golf shirts— which two are you going to
get rid of and donate? If you purchased a new pair
of sandals, which pair of shoes will you donate?

- If you have not worn or used something for 3 or 6
months, do you really need it? Let it go! Give it to
someone who could use it.

- Are your closets or kitchen cabinets filled with
things you have not used? Why not donate them to
a family recovering from a crisis?

- How many outdated products do you have in your
kitchen pantry? Or in your skin care drawer?

- Audit your garage and your attic. Are you
really going to use the things that are gathering dust (or even worse gathering creatures
who found a home in them)?

- And the paperwork! How many statements
do you really need to keep?

Downsizing Your Possessions without Moving
Editorial provided by Karen Martin,
Life Moves, LLC • www.lifemoves.com

Ideally, many of my clients would like to stay in their beloved homes forever. But that isn't always possible.

For the past six years, I have helped people through the process of moving and dispersing their unneeded personal possessions. It has made me aware of the growing phenomenon of seniors moving out of the homes in which they raised their families, and moving into condominiums, active adult communities and assisted living facilities, or moving to be near or with family members.

Moving from a family residence one has called home for decades brings with it emotional decisions. Most of the time, the move is a downsizing. Moving into a smaller place. What naturally follows is reducing the number of possessions you have accumulated over the years.

This can be overwhelming and stressful and a decision-making experience wrought with emotional turmoil. Take your time. You need to make good decisions about what to keep, what to give away, donate or discard. It is much easier to sort through your house *before* you put it on the market than rush through the process once the house sells.

"We never expected our house to sell in one day," one client told me. "Then we had to rush through the process of deciding what to keep and take with us to our new place." The cure for that situation is to start with a little advance preparation.

Start with a Plan
It may not be easy to sort through and let go of possessions collected over a lifetime, but the key is to develop a plan.

Start the sorting process early, and enjoy the journey. It takes time to make decisions and find "homes" for items you no longer need and that others can use.

Try this: Imagine that you are going to move. Have a look around. Check out each room of the house. Look at each item in the room and put it into a keep or discard category. All the things you will see in your living room, dining room, bedrooms, kitchen, hallways, bathrooms and garage are still not the sum of your possessions. Much of the rest of our "stuff" is hidden from view in attics, basements and closets. All of these rooms must be emptied. I have crawled into such places wearing a flashlight mounted on a headband to drag into the daylight boxes of items that have not seen the light of day for decades!

Thoughtful planning will give you sufficient time to make good choices about your possessions. Gifts to family members can be very rewarding, and you can benefit by seeing those donated items used and enjoyed instead of gathering dust. Instead of allowing these decisions to be emotionally draining, why not let them be empowering? Keep only your favorite and most valuable items. You will be better prepared for your move.

THE WORK

Many of my clients who have downsized are often surprised by the amount of work involved. It can be tiresome and emotionally draining, but also rewarding. Work at your own pace. You will enjoy it more if you can perform the task with loved ones, family members, or good friends at your side. Holding objects you have not seen in a long time may trigger rich stories and memories. These "good old days" are better relived with people who are close to you.

If you don't have family help, there are professional organizers and senior move managers who may be paid to assist you. Why not begin by downsizing in place—that is, reduce your possessions before a move is even on the horizon. Then, when the time comes for the move, when the time is right for you, moving will be easier and will hopefully bring new adventures into your life. You will be ready!

THE REWARDS

Taking stock of all the items you have collected over your lifetime and disposing of some of them can give you a feeling of being in control. Working at your own pace is less stressful. Preparing for a move, even though you may stay in your home for as long as you wish, makes letting go and moving on easier—for both you and your family. Having your adult children, other family members or friends help can bring all of you closer together.

My in-laws are currently preparing to move from their home of 50 years in West Hartford, Connecticut. Over the past four months, their daughter, Janis, who lives in Chicago, has flown home three times to help. Once, Janis stayed up late at night reading letters she wrote to her parents when she was a youngster, away at summer camp. The letters reminded them both of how Janis hated being away from home. She and her mother were able to laugh at how she would count down the days until she could come home. There were also old letters from boyfriends, and, of course, plenty of elementary school art.

My mother-in-law is a saver. She stashed away nearly everything her children, who are now adults, ever produced growing up. When she presented to her oldest son, Paul, a gift of a dozen special monster models he had glued together and painted as a child, he decided to keep one. He gave a few more of his favorites to his 12-year-old nephew. The rest were sold to a collector.

Reading letters, hearing stories, and discovering such mementos can instantly take you back in time and strengthen your ties to each other with new appreciation of the family home you shared.

TEN DOWNSIZING TIPS:

1. Start with personal papers and photographs. These often take the most time to read through and decide whether to keep, give to your adult children, or shred.

2. Make sure you are comfortable and have enough light. Bring over an extra lamp to help you see better.

3. Find a long portable folding table on which to spread out your items, especially if you are removing them from a closet. That way, you can work at waist height instead of bending to the floor.

4. For garbage, I like to use the sturdy 3-millimeter thick contractor bags. Hang them off the back of a chair for tossing items away. If you are in the kitchen, you can secure the bag to the dishwasher or stove front and close the door to hold them in place.

5. For organizing, I recommend using shallow, flat-top boxes, which are sturdy and stackable. You can find them in the produce section of your local supermarket. You can place items in them quickly and see what you have at a glance. They are easy to pick up and move out of the way later.

6. It takes a lot of time to sort through clothing and accessories. If you haven't worn something for two or three years, give it to people who need and will appreciate it. Local churches, synagogues and charities will accept clean, gently worn items.

7. Ask family members for help. Those who live distances away can help you during holiday time, special celebrations or visits.

8. It is a good idea to consider the weather when you go to work in attics or garages. During the summer, morning is the coolest time to go up into the attic. In winter, a sunny afternoon is best.

9. Do not have your adult children order a dumpster and just start tossing items away. An expert appraiser can determine the worth of antiques, collectibles and ephemera (papers of historical significance).

10. Most importantly, enjoy reminiscing while you read, touch and feel items you haven't seen in years. You can capture the rich history of your life's story in creative ways.

CHAPTER X

PEARLS OF WISDOM

*"You don't stop laughing when you grow old, you grow old
when you stop laughing."*

– George Bernard Shaw

AS EVIDENCED BY THE STORIES SHARED in this book, the
wisest and eldest men and women of our society have
a lot to teach us. What I have compiled here represents
merely a fragment of the many pearls of wisdom we can
receive from this group that journalist Tom Brokaw called
"the Greatest Generation"—those who grew up during the
Great Depression and saw their country through World
War II. This generation seems to have mastered the art and
science of aging with grace and dignity. They also seem
to manifest a spirit of gratitude and appreciation for every breath of life. They refuse to spend their life hoping
for what they do not have. They seem to eschew thinking about growing old. They are mentally and spiritually
tough. They don't waste their time angsting over whether
they have more wrinkles, or seeking miracle creams to keep
them looking younger. They are not chasing the elusive
Fountain of Youth. They celebrate lives well-lived and em-

brace the fulfilled quality of their years. Those who have lived past their eighties and nineties cherish the time with which God has blessed them and seek to have purposeful lives. Many of them still contribute to their communities, churches and families; they are still teaching us.

My prayer is this: that we seek out this generation, one by one, and hear their stories, learn from their memories, understand the essence of the values that laid the foundation of who they are. May we learn from them the important life lessons that can not only influence our lives, but get this great nation back to the nation they helped shape.

We are living in extraordinary times. Today's new paradigm is the new age of a much older age. Long life is not only a remarkable accomplishment, but it also imbues those who achieve it with significant wisdom—a resource from which the rest of us may draw. In the process of writing this book, it has become clear to me that aging is not exclusively a function of genetics, but also how we choose to live our lives. Genetics plays a key role, but not a secondary one to such elements as purposeful living, family ties, social connections, and lifestyle choices. What you eat, how much you exercise, and how you handle life's challenges contribute as much to your well-being and mental health as the good genes you inherited from your forebears.

With longevity now redefining every aspect of the American dream, we will need to revisit the negative connotation of a "late bloomer." We can no longer obsess about holding on to our youth. That obsession will of necessity now shift to what can you do with the next 30, 40, or even 50 years once you retire (or, is it "re-wire?"). If you retire in your sixties, and you have a 30- or 40-year retirement horizon, are you prepared to meet the next several phases of your life with a mental, emotional, physical, spiritual and financial balance? More than likely, the best songs to be composed, businesses to be started, books to be written will be a product of our later life stages, much like some of these individuals:

- *At 55, Ronald Reagan left his acting career for public office as governor of California.*
- *At 61, Helen Mirren, the British actress, won her first Academy Award for her role in "The Queen."*
- *At 62, Colonel Harland Sanders, after working odd jobs, opened the first Kentucky Fried Chicken franchise and became a national icon.*
- *At 65, Laura Ingalls Wilder published her first book in the famed "Little House" series.*
- *At 69, Mother Teresa (now Saint Teresa of Calcutta) won the Nobel Peace Prize after decades of missionary work.*
- *At 75, Grandma Moses, a celebrated artist, swapped her crochet needles for brushes and became world-famous for her paintings.*
- *At 80, Joan Didion, award-winning author, landed a modeling gig for the high-end brand Celine.*
- *At 90, Millard Kaufman, co-creator of the near-sighted cartoon character Mr. Magoo, wrote his first novel.*
- *At 96, Harry Bernstein finally achieved fame with the publication of his memoir about growing up Jewish in a small town in England.*

- *At 96, Fred Stobaugh, a retired truck driver from Peoria, Illinois, wrote his first hit song, "Oh Sweet Lorraine."*
- *At 104, Fauja Singh, a man of Punjabi Indian descent, became the first man over the age of 100 to complete a marathon.*

(Source: *Time, "Secrets of Living* Longer"; single issue magazine, 2015)

So, how do you live to be 100 and beyond? Here's a recap of the pearls of wisdom gathered from research, shared in the interviews, and from my personal experience caring for family members who lived beyond 90.

GRATITUDE

Live every day with a spirit of gratitude for everything in your life. Be grateful every morning you wake up, and cherish the blessings in your life. Appreciation for the things you have, the family connections, friends, the very simple things in life, seem to be the most critical lesson learned. In members of "The Greatest Generation," such gratitude apparently stems from an innate spirit of joy upon which their lives are built. It is not the result of some "glass half-full" versus "glass half-empty" psychology they picked up at a self-help seminar. It is part of their character and mental frame of reference. They are the generation that is simply grateful.

STAY CONNECTED TO THOSE YOU LOVE—HAVE A RICH SOCIAL NETWORK

This means staying close to your family and friends. As you relocate to different communities and locations, stay connected and have appropriate social interactions and activities. The more social engagement you have, the greater energy and joy you will have in your life. Those who live in retirement communities and have strong social interaction throughout the day, at meals and other planned activities, enjoy "active" longevity.

ADHERE TO THE PRINCIPLES OF CLEAN LIVING AND EATING RIGHT

A lifestyle of moderation lends itself to a long and healthy life. This means eating simply, and not over-indulging in food, alcohol or tobacco. A key takeaway from my interviews with those of the 90 + generation in this book was that moderation is a key to longevity. Most of them favored eating in instead of eating out, for example.

RISE ABOVE LIFE'S CHALLENGES

The ability to push through life's challenges is crucial. When problems and difficulties raise their ugly heads through each stage of life, having a positive and determined spirit seems somehow connected to longevity. The mindset of "driving through" challenges helped many of these members of the "Greatest Generation" get through and come out on top. "Do not sweat the small stuff" is a phrase that we hear often, yet we continue to spend our lives "sweating the small stuff." Many of those I interviewed had risen above such challenges as physical impairment, emotional crisis, loss of loved ones, loss of friends, and loss of mobility. Still they continued their lives with purpose and joy.

MAINTAIN AN ACTIVE LIFESTYLE

A common mantra is "keep moving." Regardless of one's age or life stage, movement is a key ingredient to longevity. While you may not be able to drive to a gym every day when you're 85 or 95, movement is key. And this applies not only to working out your physical body, but mental exercise as well. Playing board games, working on brain teasers, word puzzles, reading, coloring, artwork, crafts, etc., all contribute to a healthy, long life.

Maintain Spiritual Balance
Balance of mind, body and spirit is another key to longevity. The spiritual element does not necessarily mean a structured religious routine, although many of those living beyond 90 have a strong spiritual muscle through their active engagement in their respective church affiliations. But many had no church affiliation; they still consider themselves well-grounded spiritually because they have their own spiritual exercises in which they engage, whether it is simply reading their Bible at home, or meditating, or just reaching out to help others in need. They are giving back spiritually.

Seek to Minimize Isolation
Another common thread I saw among those who enjoyed long and healthy lives was staying engaged with others in social settings, with family, and creating an "extended family" wherever one landed. This is the generation that is constantly reaching out and touching others; staying engaged in their own lives and the lives of others.

Plan Ahead—in All Aspects
Oh my, what we can learn from these wise persons regarding planning for the future. They plan ahead. Most of them planned well for their retirement journey both financially and physically. What I mean by planning physically is that they planned where they would live when they retired, and as they grew through their life stages. They planned well, and now they don't find themselves in that uncomfortable

position of having to worry about running out of money as so many baby boomers do.

COMMIT TO TRADITIONAL VALUES

Values play a huge role in longevity and while this may not seem logical, it was evident because they value family and country unconditionally. They have something against which to hold up their lives. This gives them strength because, in their mind, they live in the greatest nation on earth, and what could be better than that? Also, holding true to what matters in life—such as family relationships, God and country—seem to play a vital role in longevity.

LIVE WITHOUT REGRETS

Absolutely NO REGRETS. Nothing on bucket lists, no unfulfilled desires or dreams. Just live your life in a purposeful and meaningful way, unencumbered by the drama of unresolved hurt, forgiveness or unfulfilled dreams. They cherish each day with which God blesses them. What a lesson for the masses!

HAVE PURPOSE: DON'T RETIRE "FROM" SOMETHING UNLESS YOU "GO TO" SOMETHING

A key ingredient to longevity is purpose and passion for life. It has nothing to do with how great that purpose or passion is. A golden rule I learned from the Greatest Generation is to never "end" something without having something with which to replace it. Don't stop a career without knowing what you're going to do next. Whether it's traveling, recreation, or building another career, have a purpose and know your next move before you make it.

EMBRACE AGING

This generation taught me that "aging" is a word that needs to be extinguished from the dictionary and our language, just like the word "retirement." They find that being "old," as society would call them, is quite nice and better than you might think. They are not old in their thinking, their activities, their involvement in their families and communities, in pursuing relationships. Some have found love again in their 80's and 90's. Isn't that a beautiful aspect of aging?

TREAT YOUR MIND AND BODY KINDLY

Another amazing lesson I learned is this: If you knew you would live to 90, 100, 110 or perhaps longer, would you treat your body or your mind like you are doing so at age 50, 60, or 70? Probably not. It's never too late to take control of your mind, your body, or your spirit. Just live life assuming you will join the ranks of the centenarians and supercentenarians. I read somewhere that you should "act now like you'll need your body for more than 100 years."

DO NOT FOCUS ON DYING— JUST LIVING

Absolutely no focus should be given to "Am I going to die?" These people know they will die someday, just like everyone else in the world. But they do not focus on it. They have a passion for life, and for living. Even when they experience a physical setback, their energy shifts to getting through it, and getting back in the game of life. It's all about living, not dying.

BE A CONTINUOUS LEARNER

Not a day goes by that they don't engage their mental capabilities. They are still learning through working, writing, going to various classes, volunteering, etc. They continue to learn and grow and they have given new meaning to the phrase "When you're green you're growing; when you're ripe, you're rotten." Don't rot; keep learning and growing.

So, here you have it, dear reader. Pearls of wisdom from the Greatest Generation in a simple snapshot that could put you on your journey to a healthy and totally vibrant life.

To those of you who volunteer to join me in the ranks of the centenarians and supercentenarians, heed these 15 pearls of wisdom and shape your future. Our nation, our families, and our businesses need the wisdom of the ages if we are to thrive. We need to continue contributing to that wisdom. It's not how much time you have left; it's about what you do with that time and the legacy you leave to the generations that follow you.

About the Author

JEANNETTE BAJALIA is president and principal advisor for Petros Estate & Retirement Planning based in Jacksonville, Florida. She is also president and founder of Woman's Worth®, a company that specializes in the unique life planning needs of women. She was born in Jacksonville and now lives a few footsteps away from the Atlantic Ocean in Ponte Vedra Beach, Florida. After more than 38 years in the corporate world, Jeannette left her executive position with Blue Cross & Blue Shield of Florida in 2007 and launched her second career as a retirement planner. Since her mission has always been to help people improve the quality of their lives through her work, she views the transition from insurance executive to retirement planner as a continuation rather than a change of direction.

Jeannette provides integrated planning and counseling on a wide range of financial issues including lifetime income planning, tax reduction strategies, estate planning and investments. She is the author of *Wi$e Up Women!—A Guide to Total Fiscal and Physical Well-Being*, published by Advantage Media Group in 2012, which brought a woman's perspective to Retirement Lifestyle Protection Planning™. She also wrote *Retirement Done Right*, published on Amazon in 2015. Her cut-to-the-chase style of communicating and her keen insight into the financial landscape of retirement challenges and solutions has garnered much attention from the media. She has been featured in *The Wall Street Journal* and *Forbes*, and was selected by *The Jacksonville Business Journal* as one of 20 "Women of Influence" of 2012. In the last few years, she has been interviewed by major TV networks and has been seen on CNBC, Reuters, Yahoo! Finance.com and MarketWatch.com. She is host of a weekly radio program, Woman's Worth® Radio, which airs on WOKV, 104.5 FM and has appeared on "First Coast Living" on WTLV. She has been published in such periodicals as *Entrepreneur Anchor* and *Health Source, Investor's Business Daily, Houston Chronicle, Newsmax* and has been featured in both *The Florida Times Union*, and the *Ponte Vedra Recorder* and is speaker for many area women's groups and professional organizations.

CAREER PATH

Jeannette began her corporate career at insurance giant Prudential on the day after she graduated from high school at age 16, and rose to a middle-management position by age 21.

"My parents could not afford for me to go to college," says Jeannette, "so I worked at Prudential in a very demanding position and went to college at night."

Jeannette earned her bachelor's degree in three years while working full time. It took her two years to get her master's degree from the University of North Florida, again while working full time.

When she left the corporate world and approached Petros Financial Services to ask about a position as an advisor, she did so out of frustration. She had approached five other "financial advisors" seeking advice on what to do with her 401(k) account and the lump sum payout of her pension plan.

"Those I approached wanted to grab my assets and put them in the stock market without any planning based on my retirement goals or risk tolerance," remembers Jeannette. "And these were high-end advisors who didn't seem to want to understand me or my plans for the future. Under their system I would have no guarantees that my money would last as long as I might live. I decided I could do a better job myself, if I only had the tools. I realized they didn't care about me. ... They only cared about my money."

Her quest led her to Petros.

"I had only intended to stick my toe into the water of financial planning, just enough to find my own solutions," Jeannette said. "But I soon became intrigued with the process. It seemed like a natural fit for me to take the training to become credentialed as a retirement advisor."

The timing was right, and in a few months, Jeannette, now fully "un-retired" and back at work, could build an integrated retirement planning approach and in two short years bought the company. She changed the business model of Petros from a firm that only did insurance sales to being a comprehensive, fully integrated retirement planning firm. And, she founded a company, Woman's Worth®, which focuses on life planning for women. Under her influence, and after purchasing Petros, she expanded to help retirees deal with retirement income strategies, estate and tax planning, healthcare solutions and insurance solutions serving Jacksonville, St. Augustine, Palm Coast, Orlando and all surrounding areas.

FAMILY LIFE

When Jeannette describes her family life, she speaks of herself as a "first-generation American." Her father and mother both immigrated to the United States and she was born here. Hers was a traditional family, deeply religious and rooted in the Middle Eastern culture.

"I saw my mother take care of my grandmother for seven years after her stroke," Jeannette remembers. "There was never a question about it. That's what family means. My father passed away when I was 26 and I ended up taking care of my mother and my aunt until they died; my mother lived to 93 and my aunt to 101."

Jeannette describes her mother and father as hard-working individuals who were the epitome of hospitality, opening their home to anyone in need. She says that they appreciated the opportunity America presented them. She has fond memories of working behind the cash register at her father's store when she was only 7 years old and getting to know loyal customers.

"They loved the Lord and made sure we knew what was expected of us with regard to upholding the family legacy," says Jeannette. "They would not allow us to abdicate the values we were raised with. They were wonderful examples of 'tough love' and were relentless in teaching us values and morals."